SECONDARY
SCHOOL
TEACHING

Problems and Methods

SECONDARY SCHOOL TEACHING
Problems and Methods

THEODORE W. HIPPLE

University of Florida
Gainesville, Florida

 GOODYEAR PUBLISHING COMPANY, INC.
Pacific Palisades, California

Library of Congress Catalog Card Number:
75–99956

Current printing (last number):
10 9 8 7 6 5

Printed in the United States of America

This volume is respectfully dedicated to three grade school children

KATHY, BRUCE, AND BETSY

with the hope that someday they may have secondary school teachers who are better prepared as a result of studying this book.

PREFACE

Intended for the instruction of prospective or relatively inexperienced teachers in junior and senior high schools, this book is based on two assumptions. The first of these is that the problems that give teachers the most difficulty, the ones that cause them to teach poorly or to leave teaching altogether, are seldom subject-matter problems. To be sure, there are those teachers for whom life in a secondary school is unpleasant or unproductive because they feel they lack the background and sophistication in their subject areas requisite for a good classroom performance. I submit, though, that such teachers are few. Far more common are those teachers—literally thousands of them—whose difficulties with such aspects of teaching as planning and motivation, as testing and evaluation, as discipline make them unsuccessful and unhappy. A high school history teacher, for example, rarely leaves teaching or teaches ineffectually because he knows too little history; rather, his efforts fall short of his desires because he cannot motivate his students to learn what he can teach them or because he cannot control his class or because he has trouble with testing or because of a host of problems which have little to do with history.

The second assumption is that prospective or inexperienced teachers can profit from an examination of problems that teachers have actually encountered; this book is mainly composed of such problems, and the format of their presentation virtually demands the kind of reader participation that I have posited as being helpful for teachers. Moreover, the cases included in this text are drawn from general areas of teaching strategy and practice like those identified in the first paragraph; they are not specifically subject-matter problems.

Each case is actually a four-page unit, with a statement of the problem on the initial page, a blank facing page on which the reader can write how he would solve the problem and why he thinks his solution would be effective, a third page—again blank—on which the reader can write his reactions to the alternate solutions presented to him on the fourth page. These solutions are presented in no particular order; they are given randomly to encourage reader attention to all of them.

Following the collections of problems on each topic is a brief overview of that topic. This is not a comprehensive statement, nor is it intended to be. Rather it is direct, sometimes blunt, advice, especially designed for the future teacher who has more questions than answers. How to motivate? What methods of presentation to use? On what to base a grade? What to do with a student who cheats?

Finally, a short bibliography completes each chapter and provides the reader anxious to explore further some of the topics an opportunity to secure additional and, not infrequently, different perspectives and suggestions.

The arrangement of the topics covered in this text implies no hierarchy of importance. For some teachers the actual classroom presentation gives them their most grievous moments; for others, discipline is a major cause of trouble; for still others, the emotional concerns of individual students become their emotional concerns, too. Thus, the order of the topics is less important than their treatment. No less a problem than the order of the topics is their interrelatedness. Motivation, for example, cannot be separated from classroom presentation or from discipline; cheating certainly has a close relationship with evaluation. The separation here, then, permits an easy examination of the topics, but should not be construed as implying a similar separability in the schools.

The problems, though, make the book. These include not only the expected discipline and testing cases but also some peculiar to ghetto schools or to team teaching arrangements. With all of these problems the prospective teachers can grapple, if only vicariously, with things that have actually happened in secondary schools. They can try their hand at solutions and can compare their responses with those provided by their colleagues. Out of such mental activity and discussion can come, I believe, teachers who are better able to cope with the problems they face when they teach, problems that may not differ much from some of these included here. If indeed they are better teachers as a result of studying these cases, then their time in reading this book and mine in writing it will have been worthwhile.

Many are the people whom I should thank for help with this volume, but chief among them are the many students, future or practicing teachers all, at the Universities of Illinois and Florida who have studied these problems and offered solutions. Our classes have been exciting because of these cases and the give-and-take discussions we have had about them. Many of these problems are ones I faced in my decade of teaching in the secondary schools and not infrequently the solutions offered by my university students were ones I wish I had thought of when I first encountered the problems. Perhaps my students' exposure to these problems in the safe shelter of the college classroom will help them react with equal confidence and ability when they teach. I hope so.

One final word seems pertinent. As an outgrowth of the work he and others did for the American Association of Colleges of Teacher Education, Professor B. O. Smith co-authored *Teaching for the Real World*, a book which I believe will profoundly influence future practices in teacher education. Speaking of his work before our College of Education faculty this fall, Professor Smith called upon us, and indeed upon all who are interested in improving the education of future teachers, to produce "protocol materials." These may include specific teaching situations, either on videotape or in printed form, which the prospective teacher may study and react to. The problems in this book provide readers a similar opportunity for study and reaction and, though prediction from the author about the usefulness of his book may be dangerous, if not arrogant, I do believe that the study and reaction of these problems will result in improved classroom performance. And that is what teacher education is all about.

THEODORE W. HIPPLE
Gainesville, Florida

CONTENTS

SECONDARY
SCHOOL
TEACHING

Problems and Methods

CHAPTER ONE

The Teacher
and
the Student

TIMOTHY IS TRYING . . . VERY TRYING

That Timothy is bright is true; that Timothy knows that he is bright is even truer. And he seems set on making you equally aware of his intelligence, even if he must ruin your physics class to do so.

You're the first to admit that physics isn't exactly your long suit. With a thin college minor and no methods courses or student teaching experiences in physics, you feel a little out of your element the one period a day you teach that subject. The math you teach the other periods of the day is going well enough, but, then, Timothy is not in those classes.

More times than you care to remember in these first eight weeks of your first year of teaching, you have been corrected as you presented your lessons, and always the corrections have come from Timothy. Though he has been courteous, Timothy has at times significantly disrupted what you felt to be a good lesson. On one occasion, for example, as you attempted to lead the class inductively through a complex lesson, Timothy interrupted and gave the final generalization you were working toward. His ability had permitted him to jump ahead, but you are certain that the other students were confused by Timothy's giant strides as they took the baby steps you had planned for them. On another occasion he broke into the presentation with the question, "Wouldn't it be simpler to understand and to teach if you approached it this way?" He then proceeded to outline a manner of presentation that was indeed better than yours, though yours would have gotten the job done.

None of the other students are in Timothy's league and with them you feel you are doing adequate work. Yet there sits Timothy, ever ready to leap in with the question he knows you cannot answer, the suggestion for change that you had not thought of in your planning, the answer to your problem before the others in the class have even figured out what the problem is. Always he is politeness itself; always his hand is raised, his voice soft, his manner kind, but his intent clear: he doesn't like the way you are teaching physics. You are beginning to wonder if Timothy's remarks are affecting the way the class views your teaching.

You have finally decided you must do something about Timothy. But what?

YOUR SOLUTION

YOUR REACTIONS TO THE ALTERNATE SOLUTIONS

ALTERNATE SOLUTIONS

1. Talk privately to Timothy about his interruptions of your physics lessons and make it plain that you'd appreciate it if he would shut up and let you muddle through as best you can.

2. Say nothing and let Timothy continue his ways. When his suggestions are appropriate, use them.

3. Create challenging extra-credit assignments for Timothy and frequently excuse him from class to work on them in the lab or in the library.

4. Seek the approval of the class members, who already know of Timothy's extraordinary ability, for appointing him your special assistant and, if granted, let him do some of the actual teaching.

THE MISERIES OF MELISSA

The prettiest thing about Melissa is her name. She is short and—there are no other words—sloppy fat. Her dresses are old and out of style and not always as clean as they could be. Nor has Melissa any academic brilliance or sparkling personality that she might use as compensation for her obvious deficiencies. In your tenth grade speech class, one of average ability, she does average work—that is, when she works at all. For she is understandably petrified about standing before the class and giving a speech. Once there she is the subject of the smirks, the giggles, even the barbed and cruel remarks of her classmates who see her as one big—very big—joke.

As Melissa's speech teacher you're beginning to wonder how far your responsibilities extend. You've been kind to her, perhaps even a little more considerate than to the other students in the class. Yet her response has been one of studied indifference, only slightly warmer than the outright contempt she displays for her fellow students. Still, you've been asking yourself if you should speak to her, perhaps tell her something of personal hygiene.

Or should you talk to the class sometime when Melissa is absent? Your relationships with them are fairly good and possibly the students would heed your remarks about friendship and about kindness to others less fortunate. In so doing, however, you might worsen the situation by making the other students think Melissa was your special pet. You could, of course, do nothing and adopt a "whatever will be, will be" attitude.

But the cruelty Melissa is subjected to, especially in your class where oral participation is a daily occurrence, almost forces you to do something. After all, you think, she is a fellow human being in trouble and you should help.

The question remains, though: How?

YOUR SOLUTION

YOUR REACTIONS TO THE ALTERNATE SOLUTIONS

ALTERNATE SOLUTIONS

1. Send Melissa from the room on some pretext (perhaps to the library for a special project) and have a pointed discussion with the rest of the class about their treatment of Melissa. Let them know that you expect different future behavior from them, at least while Melissa and they are in your class.
2. Have a frank talk with Melissa about her weight and her lack of cleanliness. Tell her you'll try to help if she wants to consider dieting.
3. Urge Melissa's counselor or the school nurse to have a talk with her.
4. Call Melissa's mother and speak to her about her daughter's problems.
5. Don't do anything. These things will work themselves out in time.

AH . . . LOVE

In your second semester of teaching chemistry in an upper-class suburban high school, you have become confident enough of your ability to control the class that you are letting your students sit wherever they please. Naturally, Bob and Sally, who you know have been going steady for months, sit near each other. Sometimes they whisper and one time you saw them pass a note, but you have taken the position that young love must have its moments and have not reprimanded them. Besides, they are both clean-cut, nice kids: Bob, the All-American-Boy type; Sally, the girl next door. They do fairly well in your course, too, partly, you believe, because they have told you that they study it together every night. Though you have no proof, you suspect that Bob and Sally may be using your course as justification to their parents for seeing each other nightly.

One day after class you are straightening the chairs when you notice a paper under Sally's desk. Picking it up to throw away, you see from the careful way it is folded that it is a note, probably from Bob to Sally. Knowing that you shouldn't read it, but being too curious to resist the temptation to see how those who go steady communicate these days, you sit at your desk and begin the note.

The note, you discover, is actually a conversation between Bob and Sally. (Apparently they were better at note-passing than you had thought.) But what bothers you is not their skill at secret communications, but rather the content of the message: The note makes it plain that Bob and Sally have been having sexual intercourse. Sally has written of her concern that she is late in her menstrual period. Bob is trying to assure her that she can't be pregnant.

Your move.

YOUR SOLUTION

YOUR REACTIONS TO THE ALTERNATE SOLUTIONS

ALTERNATE SOLUTIONS

1. Do nothing at all.* Try to forget that you have even seen the note.

2. Call in Bob or Sally or both of them, have a frank conversation about the contents of the note and ask if there is a way that you can help them.

3. Take the note to the high school counseling staff and let them decide what, if anything, to do.

4. Call Bob's parents and/or Sally's parents and tell them of the note and its contents.

5. Try to establish a closer relationship with Bob and Sally with the hope that they will confide in you and ask your help.

6. Try to get the information in the note to the ministers or priests or rabbis in the churches Bob and Sally attend and solicit their help.

---

* This is not a frivolously offered alternate solution. Not infrequently a teacher's best solution to a problem may be his inaction, his letting the problem work itself out. This, however, may not be the best solution to the present problem.

THE PURLOINED PEN AND PENCIL SET

Teaching in an inner-city school, you think, would challenge the best teacher in the history of education and, as a first-year member of the profession, that teacher you are not. Still, you do believe you have had some successes with your social problems classes.

Perhaps most notable—until today, that is—is Roy. In early September he told you that he was going to drop out of school in November. You began counseling him on an occasional basis, and before long both his school work and his attitudes toward school began to improve. Your examination of school records revealed that Roy lives in conditions of almost unbelievable poverty and that he gets no encouragement at home. You want, therefore, to give him all the attention and help you can. He is responding well, is really trying in all of his courses now. You're justifiably proud of your accomplishment and believe that he will finish high school.

Today Roy thanked you for your help—with a gift of a beautiful pen and pencil set still in its original box. After thanking him, you gently questioned whether the gift was too expensive for him to afford.

"No, that's all right," he replied, perhaps just a bit evasively.

When you pushed the issue, Roy became distrubed and angry. Finally he blurted out, "Look, if you don't want the stuff, throw it away. It doesn't matter to me; I didn't pay nothing for it."

Yes, Roy stole the pen and pencil set from some store. What, if anything, do you do now?

YOUR SOLUTION

YOUR REACTIONS TO THE ALTERNATE SOLUTIONS

ALTERNATE SOLUTIONS

1. Thank Roy for his gift and regard it as just that—a gift, regardless of what you know about its source. Begin to use the pen and pencil, especially when Roy is around.

2. Tell Roy that school policy forbids teachers' accepting gifts from students. Suggest that he return the gift to the store for a "refund," hoping that he'll get the hint and sneak the set back to the store from which he stole it.

3. Take Roy's name, the pen and pencil, and your suspicions to the school principal and let him decide on future actions.

4. Tell Roy that you know he stole the set and try to talk with him about the theft. Urge him to return the pen and pencil and to steal no more.

THE UBIQUITOUS EILEEN

In a class you had taken in college you'd learned that some junior high and senior high school students crave attention, but nothing had quite prepared you for Eileen in your eighth grade English class. She obviously worships the very classroom floor you walk on and will do anything she can to secure your attention and approval. When papers need distributing, when a window has to be raised, when the chalkboard needs erasing, there is Eileen, wildly swinging her arm and begging that you choose her for the task.

At the beginning of the year, your first in teaching, you often did call on her for these duties and were pleased at Eileen's display of enthusiasm for you and your course. Now, though, you are wondering if these early gestures haven't backfired.

Eileen wants to answer every question you ask and often just blurts out the response; frequently she is wrong, but your gentleness in handling her incorrect answers has only added to her feelings about you. She is at your door when you get to school in the morning, is in your room every night after school. You are beginning to believe Shakespeare's adage, "Familiarity breeds contempt," and are feeling guilty about your occasional hopes that Eileen will be absent or will get transferred or will start hating you.

Yet her actions do have some justification, perhaps. Your check with the school records revealed that Eileen is a middle child in a family of eleven children. Both her father and her mother work and doubtlessly they are unable to give each of their children the attention which they would want to extend to them and which Eileen so desperately needs. You've asked her other teachers and learned from them that Eileen's attention-getting is confined to you and your class. No wonder, you think; she hasn't time to see her other teachers.

Her reasons notwithstanding, Eileen is getting to be something of a problem. Her before- and after-school appearances make difficult your talking with students who need your help. Her dominating, or trying to dominate, classroom activities has turned many of what you thought would be full class discussions into two-man dialogues.

You must, you decide, take some action. The next decision, though, is the harder one: What action are you going to take?

YOUR SOLUTION

YOUR REACTIONS TO THE ALTERNATE SOLUTIONS

ALTERNATE SOLUTIONS

1. Simply tell Eileen, kindly but firmly, that you have other students who have legitimate demands on your time and that she'll have to stop coming to your room so often before and after school and also stop monopolizing classroom activities.

2. See Eileen's counselor and her other teachers, tell them your problem, and urge them to show Eileen a little more interest in the hope that they will be able to supply some of the attention she needs.

3. Let things continue as they are. As one of eleven children, Eileen deserves your attention, even if giving it means some problems for you.

4. Begin to ignore Eileen. Don't call on her for any of the tasks she's so fond of doing, reprimand her for interrupting class, be very cool with her before and after school. Move into this program gradually, hoping that before long she'll get the hint.

KNOWING THE STUDENTS

Teaching in the secondary schools is best regarded as a ternary process: X teaches Y to Z. You, the X, if you are to be a successful teacher, must pay extensive attention to *both* elements in the process besides yourself. A consideration of Y, the subject being taught, the element that teachers all too often stress to the point of ignoring the others, is beyond the purview of a book on general education; a consideration of Z, the students, is not. The good teacher knows his students and knows them well, not necessarily as friends or enemies but as individual people to whom he has special responsibilities and on whom he exerts, for good or ill, an influence that is far more pervasive than that imparted alone by the subject he teaches.

If yours is the career of the typical teacher, you can legitimately expect that some of your students will love you, but others may despise you; some will find you the most enthusiastic of teachers, but others may think you dull beyond description; some will delight in their opportunity to share your knowledge about a subject they are interested in, but others may wonder if your attachment for that subject does not offer *prima facie* evidence of a deficiency in your mental equipment. These dichotomies could continue, but to little point, for the ultimate generalization remains the same: the students you teach will not all regard you in the same way.

Similarly, you should not think of them as "one," but rather as individuals whom you should try to get to know as well as you are able. While it is obvious that your students are different, it is also unfortunately obvious that many secondary school teachers ignore these differences and teach as though all their students were the same. Their teaching may be satisfactory; if, however, they were to use in their teaching what they know or could learn about their students, that teaching could become outstanding.

You will discover the truth of this statement—that the better you know your students, the better teacher you are likely to be—each day you are in the classroom. For, on each of these days, you will get to know a little bit more about one or two students: their reactions to being praised, for example, or their concern about a provocative discussion question you have raised. These little pieces of information, taken cumulatively, can provide quite a sizable fund of information, information that will help you teach your students, and, more importantly, teach them as the individuals they are.

A student, too, benefits when he sees himself being regarded by his teachers as an individual. As secondary schools grow in size, the lament often heard at large universities—"I'm not a person, I'm just a number"— may become common at junior and senior high schools. When a student feels, though, that at least one of his teachers (but preferably all of them) knows him well enough to greet him by name not only in the classroom but also in the halls between periods, at the basketball game on Friday night, at church on Sunday morning, that student's attitudes about school and teachers may become good ones, the kind he must have if he is to learn effectively.

The best way, of course, for you to come to know your students is to teach them—provided, that is, that your teaching is not the day-after-day lecture that could just as easily be given in a vacuum or to a group four times the size of your class. If you have frequent class participation— recitations, discussions, group activities, panels, etc.—you will learn about the individual students quickly. Betty, who speaks with an unmistakable but difficult to categorize accent; Howard, who mentions his being on the football team every chance he gets; Susan, who is brilliant at finding flaws in others' arguments, including yours; Tommy, who is shy, withdrawn, reluctant to recite—these students and all of their classmates spring suddenly to life, take shape, and become for you what they in fact are— individual human beings.

The use of specific names above is not unintentional. Do endeavor to learn the names of your students as soon as possible. With as many as 175 different students to teach, this task is difficult, but you can make it easier by creating and using a seating chart. Your use of such a chart does not mean that you must use the traditional alphabetical arrangement of students. You can still permit students to sit wherever they like or can seat them on some sort of lottery basis; your only stipulation is that they remain in the seats assigned them until you have learned their names.

Another common way to become acquainted with your students is to examine their permanent records. In most schools each student has an individual cumulative folder that travels with him from grade to grade and from school to school; it includes such information as past grades, standardized test scores, comments from previous teachers, attendance records, parents' occupations, and the like. Usually kept in the guidance offices of the school, these records are generally available for teacher examination. When used properly, they can be a source of much valuable information. You can discover, for example, that Sharon's having moved six times in the first seven grades may have something to do with the intense shyness she exhibits in your class. Jerry's difficulty with the textbook you've assigned him may become more understandable after your discovery that his reading level is several years below his grade level.

Used improperly, however, these records can be injurious to your students. The Bob the fifth grade teacher labeled a failure may not be the same Bob you're presently teaching in the tenth grade. Even such normally reliable indicators as scores on standardized tests must be considered as part of a total, and much larger, picture of the student and never in isolation. A student may have been ill when he took the test, he may have misunderstood the directions, he may have mismarked his answer sheet— any of these could have resulted in his having a score in his folder that does not accurately reflect his present ability or achievement.

Perhaps the best attitude to take with respect to cumulative folders is that they serve better to provide corroborative, rather than predictive, data. If you believe that Johnny's difficulties with your course stem from a reading problem, you may be able to secure information about his reading from his folder. Seeing the record first may predispose you to see Johnny as a poor reader when, in fact, the deficiencies that caused the low score in his records have long since been removed.

Another way of getting to know your students is to attend some of the extraclass activities of the school. Pay attention to which of your students are school athletes, debaters, cheerleaders, thespians, musicians. You will not have the time, of course, to attend every athletic event, every school play, every band concert, but do try to get to some of them. For information about those activities you cannot attend, the school newspaper can be a good source, as can the school yearbook from the previous year.

As stated above, once you know students as individuals, teaching them becomes easier and more likely to be productive of optimal success. You can create individual assignments that are truly individual. You can call on a student in class by name and with assurance that this person is the right one for the question you have asked. You can form intraclass groups with social purposes, as well as academic ones, guiding your choices. Putting all the shy students in one group tends sometimes to relieve their tension and draw all of them out. Creating groups of mixed intelligences in which the bright help the less intelligent can become almost routine if you know your students well. Taking advantage of special talents—Barb's first place in the school art show may make her the logical choice to head the bulletin board team, Al's position in the student government may cause you to select him to lead class discussion—can help you make your class exciting and dynamic, a class in which students, treated and respected as individuals possessing worth and dignity, will work to learn.

One more facet of your knowing well the students you teach merits treatment in this brief section, and that is your role as a guidance worker. Although the school in which you teach probably has some full-time well-trained guidance people, you still have a guidance function. Some students are going to come to you with their problems; others simply want someone friendly to talk to; still others seek out teachers to serve as advisers on matters ranging from post-high school plans to parental relationships. In many instances your best means of helping these youth is by doing what you would do anyway as a good teacher: Listen to them and talk to them. Forget about whether it is teaching or guidance. (Indeed, attempting to make a distinction between guidance and teaching could set off a debate that would take many more pages than we have here.) Your simply listening sympathetically and attentively to the students may provide them the help they most need to solve their problems. At times, of course, you may have very specific advice that you want to offer, but don't feel that you must provide a solution to every student's problem. His learning to solve his own difficulties may be as important as anything he learns in his secondary school years.

On occasion, however, you may encounter a problem of a magnitude that is beyond your solution, that requires the attention of a trained guidance worker. Three things are in order in such instances: (1) Try to get the student to see his counselor, even if this means that you must take the student yourself. (2) Make a statement yourself to the counselor, adding what you know of the problem and any other information you think pertinent; just as teachers depend upon guidance workers for information, so also do guidance workers welcome salient information from the class-room teacher. (3) Maintain some emotional distance. Becoming too involved in a student's problems, some of which the school simply cannot solve, can drain you emotionally and make you less able to perform the classroom duties that must receive your first attention. In such serious instances your getting the student to the counselor as soon as possible and informing that counselor of what you know about the matter may be crucial in helping solve the problem.

Your role in guidance goes beyond that of helping individual students. As a teacher you have certain responsibilities to the success of the guidance program. Be careful with records and data you have placed in a student's folder, but do include information that will be helpful to the student's later teachers. If you learn something about a student that you think all his teachers should know—her parents have just completed a very sticky divorce, or his Saturday job now requires that he work several nights a week as well—tell the counselor who has channels set up to pass this kind of information to the student's other teachers. In sum, if you can envision yourself and the guidance worker as full teammates in an important enterprise, namely the education of individual youths, your lot will be the easier, your teaching the better, and your students the happier for your efforts.

FOR FURTHER READING

Brammer, L. M., "The Coming Revolt of High School Students," *Bulletin of the National Association of Secondary School Principals*, 52, Sept. 1968, 13-21.

Clark, Leonard, and Irving S. Starr, *Secondary School Teaching Methods* (2nd ed.), Chap. 2. New York: The Macmillan Company, 1967.

Coleman, James, *The Adolescent Society*. New York: The Free Press, 1963.

Corey, Stephen M., "The Poor Scholar's Soliloquy," *Childhood Education*, 20, Jan. 1944, 5.

Dumas, Wayne, and Weldon Beckner, *Introduction to Secondary Education: A Foundations Approach*, Chap. 4. Scranton, Pa.: International Textbook Company, 1968.

Hoover, Kenneth H., *Learning and Teaching in the Secondary School*, Chap. 1. Boston: Allyn and Bacon, Inc., 1964.

Jersild, Arthur T., *The Psychology of Adolescence* (2nd ed.). New York: The Macmillan Company, 1963.

Oliva, Peter F., *The Secondary School Today*, Chaps. 13, 14, 15. New York: World Publishing Company, 1967.

Storen, Helen F., *The Disadvantaged Early Adolescent: More Effective Teaching*. New York: McGraw-Hill Book Company, 1968.

CHAPTER TWO

The Teacher and Planning, Motivating, and Presenting

HERE TODAY, GONE TOMORROW

You anticipated many problems before beginning your first year in the inner-city school located in the city's worst ghetto, but you did not think that attendance would be the worst of these. After four weeks of teaching algebra, however, you believe that you are about twenty days behind.

In one of your classes, a typical one, you have thirty-six students enrolled, yet the largest session you have taught had only twenty-five students and some classes have had as few as eleven. Moreover, the same students are not absent for several consecutive days (as they might be if they were sick), but come and go on a hit-or-miss basis. Thus, on one day you might present material to seventeen students; on the next day nine of the seventeen have returned, along with twelve different students. The third day six of the original seventeen and nine of the second day's twelve show up, but there are also five faces you haven't seen for several days.

You realize that these attendance problems demand some changes in your teaching, but you're not quite certain what changes to make. What are you going to do?

YOUR SOLUTION

YOUR REACTIONS TO THE ALTERNATE SOLUTIONS

ALTERNATE SOLUTIONS

1. Continue teaching as you are, presenting a lesson each day. What the absent students miss, they must make up on their own or fail.

2. Turn each day's lesson into a laboratory session and let students work on a series of daily assignments. Each returning student will begin where he stopped before his last absence.

3. Discuss with your class the problems their lack of attendance is causing and ask them for solutions.

4. Try to revise the course so that it lacks its traditional cumulative aspect. Try to make each day's lesson a separate unit that can be taught on that day without the students having had much prior information.

NO ROOM FOR WILLIAM

You have discovered that homogeneous grouping is not without problems. Your tenth grade world history class is a teacher's dream—almost. An honors section, all the students are bright, highly motivated, anxious to succeed, and willing to work hard to succeed. All, that is, except William, who has none of these attributes. He is a poor reader, an even poorer writer, and gives abundant evidence of a considerable disdain for history.

Your attempts to get William transferred into another class failed because yours is the only world history class offered second period and second period is the only time William can take the required world history course. William's counselor is as unhappy about the situation as you are, but can offer no solutions beyond "Well, do what you can for him."

What you can do probably won't help. As things presently stand, William cannot possibly pass your course legitimately, even with all kinds of special help that you haven't the time to give him. He needs different materials, different assignments, different tests, but these, too, even if available, might not be sufficient unless he adopted a different outlook about his work in your class. You are reluctant to see him doomed to failure almost from the start of the course and wonder if there isn't something you could do to give William at least a chance of passing.

Is there something you could do? If so, what?

YOUR SOLUTION

YOUR REACTIONS TO THE ALTERNATE SOLUTIONS

ALTERNATE SOLUTIONS

1. No, there is nothing you can do. If William cannot do passing work in the course to which he has been assigned, then he must fail, however sad that result would be.

2. Make William's world history course a different one from the usual honors course. Send him daily to the library to work on special assignments. Let him know that you are willing to do the extra work this modification entails, but only if he will work. If not, he can flunk.

3. Let William remain in your class, absorbing whatever he can by whatever means he can and give him a gift "D" if he tries just a little bit.

4. Tell William what the situation is and suggest that he design a year-long project (the reading of certain books that he can handle, the regular reading of a newspaper and viewing of television newscasts, the study of encyclopedia entries on topics similar to those in your course, etc.) and submit it to you for approval for credit in lieu of his completion of the typical course.

PRINCIPAL OR PRINCIPLE

Having been assigned the senior mathematics seminar for the very brightest students in the school, you determined that you would make the course as challenging as you could. Thus, you have given difficult assignments, have designed hard tests, and have graded very stringently. You have been a little disturbed that some of your students have complained about the work and about their grades, but believe still that these intelligent seniors need to face the kinds of challenges you are confronting them with before they go on to college next year.

At the end of the first marking period you averaged the grades and gave the following term marks to your nineteen students: 2 "A's," 4 "B's," 11 "C's," and 2 "D's." One week later your principal asked to see you and told you, rather bluntly, that your grades were much too low for the caliber of the students you have. These students, he explained, are all honors students, have excellent school records, and simply do not earn "C's" or "D's."

You tried to defend yourself by citing the high standards you have for the course and the demanding work you require, but your principal would have none of it. High standards, he said, are fine, but there must be a reasonable limit. Finally he said rather explicitly, but not exactly as an order, that you should revise your teaching practices or your grading practices so that your students receive higher grades. You asked for time to consider his request and are now faced with the question of your next step.

YOUR SOLUTION

YOUR REACTIONS TO THE ALTERNATE SOLUTIONS

ALTERNATE SOLUTIONS

1. Put principle ahead of principal. Submit your resignation effective at the end of the year and continue to grade as you have been, believing that over the long haul your students will appreciate what you have done.

2. Your principal is right. Do revise your standards and practices so that your students receive higher grades. Shorten your assignments, make your tests easier, be less demanding on classroom work.

3. Write letters to the superintendent of schools and to the teachers' organizations apprising them of the whole situation and complaining about your principal's high-handedness.

4. Discuss the conversation you had with your principal with the members of your class and solicit their advice. If they, on the whole, seem satisfied with the course and with your grading, stay with the system you have established. Conversely, if they seem to agree with the principal, alter the course and lower your standards for grading.

5. Try to effect a compromise with the principal. Tell him that you will see to it that any student who works hard will get at least a "C," but that "A's" and "B's" are going to continue to be awarded only to those who do exceptional work.

STRIKE ONE—AND YOU MAY BE OUT

Your economics class has been an exciting one all year. The students, all of them bright seniors, have had fun in class, have been boisterous, but they have learned well. They are interested in the material, do well on tests and assignments, and have generally been a source of satisfaction to you in your first year of teaching.

Still, it is not without some trepidation that you agree to let your department chairman visit the class. The chairman is very formal, very stiff, very businesslike—all the things your class is not; yet she has a good reputation as a teacher.

You intended saying something yesterday to your class about the impending evaluative observation and hoped that such a comment would help keep things in some semblance of order. But you forgot to. You and your class were so wrapped up in your study of the labor movement that your message about Miss Herbert's visit never did get delivered. You were still able to rest easy last night, though, because you had given an extensive written assignment which would serve you well for most of the period you're being observed. And you also have a good tight lesson prepared for the class.

But just now when you and Miss Herbert walked into the room, you knew immediately that something was wrong. All of the students were moving and talking, even more noisily than usual. And one was standing on a desk making a speech to a small group of students. Several students, you saw, had signs they were holding aloft. And then it hit you: Your students are on strike.

Grimly you look from the class to Miss Herbert, whose back seems a little bit straighter (if that is possible). A student thrusts a petition into your hand that announces (1) that no homework has been done for today, (2) that none will be done until the students get more voice in classroom activities and assignments, and (3) that students will continue to picket until they obtain certain guarantees that will be explained to you later by the class grievance committee.

As you read the petition, the class settles down somewhat, awaiting your reaction. So, you notice, does Miss Herbert. What are you going to do?

YOUR SOLUTION

YOUR REATIONS TO THE ALTERNATE SOLUTIONS

ALTERNATE SOLUTIONS

1. Scrap your planned lesson. Read the petition to the class and ask them for the report from their grievance committee. In other words, try to capitalize on their enthusiasm and let the strike discussion go on. Explain later to Miss Herbert why you did what you did.

2. Send the noisiest students and those carrying signs to the office of the disciplinarian and then try to carry on class as you had planned to.

3. Tell the class to drop the strike nonsense and to get their homework out. If they really haven't done it, give them some time to do it.

4. Tell the class that you will examine their grievance report later, but, for the moment, they must go ahead with the planned lesson as the best means of showing Miss Herbert what they have learned about economics.

ALAS! MY MELTING POT BOILETH OVER

The animosities are so thick in your lower-ability social studies class that you could cut them with the knife you would be able to borrow from almost any of your students. The Negroes in your class don't get along with the Puerto Ricans who don't like the whites who don't like the Negroes, etc. And even within the ethnic groups themselves exists a degree of bitterness you had not dreamed you would find when you took the position in this inner city school.

Your original goal to teach these students something about the history of the United States you have long since discarded. They are, you think, living their history daily in their poverty-ridden neighborhoods. Their gangs are involved in wars as fierce as those they could hear about in your class. What point to tell them of the inventions of Ben Franklin or Thomas Edison; they're more interested in the latest device for removing hubcaps or in the newest homemade gun.

Instead of taking a textbook chronological approach to history, you'd like to use the daily newspapers and weekly news magazines and current television shows to stimulate some interests in your students beyond those they acquire in their sordid ghetto existence. Already you have secured permission from your administrative superiors to make this alteration in the course and have begun gathering materials.

But before you can accomplish anything, you have to do something about the classroom volatility. The open hostility, the frequent fights or near-fights, the hateful remarks—these have to stop if your new methods are going to work.

How can you change the classroom into one that has the kind of atmosphere necessary for successful teaching?

YOUR SOLUTION

YOUR REACTIONS TO THE ALTERNATE SOLUTIONS

ALTERNATE SOLUTIONS

1. Just try to continue with your revised course as though these animosities didn't exist.

2. Talk with the students about the problems their open hostility is causing and try to get them to help effect solutions.

3. Create some structured group assignments and use ethnically mixed groups.

4. Give everyone individual assignments to complete, thus cutting down on classroom interaction and on the possibility of fighting.

5. Group the students according to ethnic origins and try to stimulate each group to outdo the others.

PLANNING, MOTIVATING, AND PRESENTING

There are numerous important aspects of the work a teacher does, but few are greater determiners of success than planning, motivating, and presenting. How you plan what you want your students to learn, how you motivate them to learn it, and how you present it so that they may learn it are too crucial to be left to chance; you owe it to yourself and to your students to consider well each of these elements of teaching.

PLANNING

The planning for their teaching that most teachers do may be classified along temporal lines: year or course planning, covering the entire year or the complete course; unit planning, covering a topic or an aspect of a course that will comprise about one to three or four weeks of teaching; and daily planning, covering the lesson of a single period. Because year and unit plans can be discussed best in terms of a specific subject like English or biology, they will be treated only briefly here; more attention will be given to the structuring of a daily lesson, an aspect of teaching so important that it alone can contribute significantly to your success or failure as a teacher.

Let us begin with some general principles of unit and course planning. It is in these kinds of long-range plans that you will need to pay much attention to the goals of your course or unit. What kinds of things do you want your students to learn? What sorts of activities will you engage them in? What kinds of behavioral changes do you hope your course or unit will effect? One question you will have to face deals with the amount of student involvement in the planning, in the setting of goals, in answering just such questions as those raised above. When students actively participate in deciding about plans for a course or unit, there may be a residue of commitment, a kind of psychological ownership of the course or unit that can have salutary effects in your teaching: students will work harder on something they have had a voice in. Teacher-made plans and goals, on the other hand, can be just as effective insofar as they are understood and accepted by the students. In some instances, too, departmental or school policies suggest the aims a specific course or unit must strive to achieve.

Whatever their source, the goals you will consider for the courses and units you design can probably be classed into the three following divisions:

Conceptual. Sometimes labeled the "cognitive objectives" or "know that" objectives, these goals refer usually to facts or understandings you wish your students to possess at the end of the course. To know that Columbus discovered America in 1492, to understand the differences between communism and socialism, to know that the sum of the angles of a triangle equals 180°, to see the relationship between a man's ambition and his behavior as one of the major themes of *Macbeth*—these are conceptual goals.

Some teachers fall into the trap of believing that the only, or at least the most efficient, way of achieving such objectives is by employing the lecture method of teaching. Yet often the facts and understandings students learn through inductive methods, through trial and error, through their own library or laboratory research, will be more thoroughly and lastingly learned. (The lecture method will be discussed at greater length in a later portion of this chapter.)

Skills. The skills goals are sometimes referred to as "know how" objectives; with these, your hope is that your students will be able to do certain tasks at the end of the course or unit. To conjugate a Latin verb, to bisect an angle, to develop a paragraph by means of examples, to dribble a basketball—these are skills goals.

Allowing your students to learn by doing is good advice with these kinds of goals. The girl whom you want to teach to type can hardly learn how if she never gets near a typewriter. But the attainment of the skills objectives does not completely preclude lecture or discussion lessons and demand, in their place, only "learn by doing" activities. Not infrequently, a student acquires a skill only after exposure to a demonstration of it, a demonstration that can be given in a lecture format.

Attitudinal. The attitudinal, or affective, goals are those which, as the name implies, involve attitudes, values, feelings. To have an appreciation of literature, to be tolerant of the opinions of others, to respect people of different backgrounds—these are examples of attitudinal goals.

The relationship between the achievement of these attitudinal goals and the classroom methods you will use to effect that achievement is by no means clear cut. These objectives are probably best met by indirection, by incorporating them into the teaching you do to accomplish the conceptual or skills goals discussed above. Teaching directly for attitudinal aims risks becoming preaching and, as millions of parents of adolescents can attest, preaching seldom produces the desired results in secondary school students. To deal with a specific example, let us return to the appreciation of good literature mentioned in the paragraph above. The teacher who so devises his lessons that his students understand the complexity of Shakespearean characterization in *Hamlet* (a conceptual goal) may, at the same time, be helping his students acquire an appreciation of Shakespeare (an attitudinal objective).

The setting of goals, then, is an important part of course and unit planning. Equally important is the determination of time allowances. United States History courses, arranged chronologically, are notorious for failing to get past World War I. Though their manifestations may be less obvious, improper time allotments are as grievous and as frequent in virtually all other subjects: the English teacher has to drop one of the major works he planned to teach, the math teacher has to teach three topics in one week after spending most of the year devoting two weeks to each topic. On a less grand scale the same kinds of weaknesses crop up in unit plans: the two-week unit somehow ends up taking four weeks. Very often the reason for such difficulties lies in a teacher's forgetting to allow for the many unexpected interruptions that plague the calendar of virtually every school. A snowstorm closes school for three days, the heating system breaks down, there is an assembly program that was announced months earlier but then forgotten by everyone but those directly involved, 60 percent of the students get the flu and are absent. Such interruptions as these can quite obviously not be planned for; your best move, therefore, is to create year and unit plans that are flexible enough to permit you some margin for disruptions in your time schedule.

Another problem you may encounter in your devising of course and unit plans is an overreliance on the textbook you intend to use. It may well be that the textbook offers an arrangement of content similar to the one you would have devised without a text; more commonly, however, the teacher lets the text dictate the course or unit. This is not a good idea. The textbook is simply one more instructional tool, albeit an important one. To make it the master relegates you and your students to the position of slaves and ought not to be done without serious consideration of the "fit" between the text and the course or unit you want.

Time and textbook problems aside, course and unit plans can give you the sense of direction and sequence necessary to insure your feeling that your teaching is purposeful. Whether in great detail or simply sketched out, this advance planning lets you (and your students) see the whole course, or a large portion of it, at one time. You can see how the parts fit together, examine the relationships between one day's lesson and the next, consider how your course fits into the total school program. Course and unit plans, then, are essential if a teacher wishes to teach as effectively as possible.

But even more important in the determination of the effectiveness of what a teacher does is the daily lesson plan, at once the most difficult and the most necessary of all the planning. On the daily lesson rests the success of all the other planning.

You have doubtlessly known teachers who taught well and seemingly did so with few, if any, daily lesson plans. They seldom referred to notes at their desks or to other previously prepared materials; they seemed always to know what they wanted to do next. This lack of apparent planning, however, should not imply that these teachers did no planning at all. Indeed, if they were good teachers, they almost certainly did daily planning, though the results of that planning may not have been put on paper. Very rare is the ad-lib teacher who teaches well every day without having done some previous planning. What these teachers had in place of specific notes was experience; they had taught the material before and were able to rely on plans they had made in earlier years. Moreover, experienced teachers develop a facility for planning at unorthodox times, while driving to school or combing their hair, and these plans they retain and employ in the classroom, even if they have not written them down.

Theirs is a practice, however, which you should not try to emulate until your experience matches theirs. As a beginning or relatively inexperienced teacher, you are well advised to make daily lesson plans, the value of which you will come more and more to respect the longer you teach.

Probably the best outlook for you to adopt toward lesson plans is that they are notes to yourself, little reminders of things you want to do, points you specifically want covered in class, activities you want your students to engage in, materials you will need for the lesson of a particular day. The daily lesson plans you design will vary in their content, but usually you should include some mention of the methods you want to use, the materials you will need, the next assignment you wish to give, and any evaluative data you may want to receive.

The amount of detail in any lesson plan also varies. The more experienced teacher, with a veritable wealth of questions to ask on a topic he has often taught in past years, may get by with a simple "Discuss" as his methodological procedure for the day. He knows the questions that keep the discussion pointed in the right way, the manner of moving from the discussion to some other activity.

As a less experienced teacher you will lack this repertory of knowledges and techniques and will be wise, therefore, to specify in some detail what you are going to do. To continue with the discussion example used in the preceding paragraph, you may want to include the questions you intend using to begin the discussion, the specific points you hope to elicit, some method you can use to summarize. You may wish to consider in your planning the role you will play in the discussion. It is good practice to have more questions than you will need, just in case the discussion proves less lively than you would like it to be. In sum, you can soon discover that there is a high correlation between how well and in what detail you plan your daily lesson and the effectiveness of that lesson.

Another aspect of structuring the daily lesson, though one often overlooked by most teachers, including those with years of experience, is a consideration of how the lesson will strike the students. If you can envision yourself as one of your students and ask "How would I like this lesson? What would I learn from it?" you can avoid possible difficulties before they arise. For example, if you suspected that, as a student, you would be made uncomfortable by a discussion on *Huck Finn* which probed black-white relationships, you might choose to alter your plans to exclude that activity.

One more aspect needs to be mentioned in this brief overview of planning. Often the planning a teacher does is that required of him by his administrative superiors. If the teacher resents this request, if he sees it as administrative nit-picking or nosiness, then he may not see his plans as having much worth to him; they are only his response to a requirement. A better approach for him, and for you, to follow is to look upon the plans as helps in teaching; if you have to "turn in" copies, so be it. The plans—course, unit, and single lesson—should still be done for the benefit of you and your students and only secondarily for your administrative superiors.

MOTIVATING

Perhaps the most important single factor in determining how well a student achieves in school or in a course is that intangible called motivation. Every teacher of a few years' experience can name at least one student of average ability who achieved on a level that was far above average; the reason for that overachievement probably was that the student was highly motivated. One of the sadder situations you will encounter in your own teaching is that of the student whose motivation to succeed so far outstrips his ability to do so that school becomes for him a continual round of frustration. Equally disturbing (and, if the good of society is considered, perhaps even more so) is the student who possesses the ability to do great things, to benefit mankind in significant ways, but who is not motivated at all in educationally desirable ways.

It has become almost a cliché in education to suggest to teachers that they begin where the students are. Yet, as with many clichés, its currency sometimes masks the important truth embodied in it. In terms of the subject content you teach, the truth is obvious: you cannot teach a student who cannot add to use the quadratic formula to solve a mathematics problem. But starting where the students are also has important implications for the subject of motivation.

Beginning where the students are permits you to provide them with the kinds of success experiences that are themselves the source of motivation. He spoke true who first said, "Nothing succeeds like success." When your students do something well, they will be willing, possibly even anxious, to do further work and continue to earn the satisfaction that follows success. Motivation, then, is built right into the classroom program. This knife cuts both ways, however, and that is why it is important that you attempt to correlate closely your requirements and the abilities of your students. If they are unable to do something, if they rightly feel that it is beyond their ability, they will very soon become frustrated and discouraged and the quality of their performance will drop. Nothing fails like failure. Therefore, your taking your students where you find them can be of crucial importance.

As suggested, past successes and failures motivate, but so also do other matters. Of one thing in teaching you may be certain: Your students will be motivated. Some of them, however, will be motivated toward goals not consonant with those you would choose for them. Ideally, you want to try to effect the kind of relationship in which their motives and yours for them become, if not one, then at least similar enough so that you are all pulling together in a direction you all consider an appropriate one. To create this relationship, you must first know something about what motivates the secondary school youth whom you teach.

Fault the educational system if you will or parents or college admissions policies, the fact remains that, for most students, the greatest single motivating force in our schools at the present time is grades. Though we might wish it were not so, the desire to get satisfactory grades stimulates most students far more than an inherent desire to learn or an all-consuming interest in a subject. Once armed with this assertion of the obvious, you should exercise care to use it, but not to exploit it. A judicious use of grades as motivating devices is quite appropriate; a disproportionate emphasis on grades only serves to entrench more deeply their importance and to move us farther from the more acceptable goals of increased learning and improved behavior.

This emphasis your students will place on grades cuts deeper into this whole area of motivation than at first it might seem. The grades themselves are but symbols, but, to your students, these symbols are the means of satisfying other desires which are important motivators, too. A student may be motivated to get the praise of his parents (or avoid their punishment); to do so, he thinks he must have good grades. He may want the recognition (honor roll, National Honor Society) that accompanies superior marks. He may want peer approval. All of these are motives in his school life, motives he sees as being satisfied when he maintains certain grade levels.

If you can broaden his perspective, can help him understand that he can attain his ends by means other than working for grades alone, you may be well on your way to changing his behavior in positive ways. This is not to say that you must convince him to get poor grades or to ignore grades altogether; rather, it suggests that you help him see that grades are but symbols, that he can earn the parental approval, the school recognition, the peer acceptance he wants in other ways which, over the long haul, will be worth more to him than the grades alone.

It is, of course, easier for me to write about your underplaying grades (but not kicking them off the team entirely) than it is for you to create the classroom environment in which grades are subordinate to other concerns. Many well-intentioned teachers want to minimize the importance of grades but, in fact, maximize their place. If you tell students that grades are not important and then, in the next breath, tell them that they must do thus-and-so or they will fail, your actual behavior belies your stated philosophy. There must be some reasons other than grades for doing thus-and-so. (Else why do it?) Stress these, too. In other words the greater the number of desirable reasons for accomplishing a task or learning a skill, the smaller the emphasis on grades.

Despite the length of the foregoing discussion of grades, other motivating factors play key roles in affecting student behavior. Some secondary school students are very much interested in learning more about a subject. Others like learning (anything) for the sake of learning (anything). For some students the competitive aspects of school are stimulating. To some students, and for the good teacher their number is relatively large, winning the approval of the teacher can be a strong motivating force. It is the wise teacher who tries to use these other motivators as helps toward the achievement of the objectives he has for his students.

This discussion has so far centered primarily on the motives students have when they enter a classroom, and it suggests again the importance of your knowing your students. In the typical junior or senior high school, it is common for a teacher to have 150 or more students; getting to know them is more than an overnight task. Thus, it may prove helpful to have these eight principles of teacher behavior to consider as you are getting acquainted with your students:

(1) First of all, if you want your students to be interested in your subject and not just in the grades they hope to earn in it, *you* must demonstrate an interest in it. The best means of achieving this display involves more than telling your students you are interested in what you teach ("Oh, I just *love* Wordsworth's sonnets."). Rather, show them that you are a person interested in many facets of life, among which is the subject you are teaching. By so doing, you let them see that out of these many interests you deliberately selected the subject which you are teaching. They may, in turn, extend you the courtesy of examining that subject to determine if it holds a similar excitement for them.

How do you demonstrate that you have a variety of interests? The best method is simply to display them, even if this procedure involves your having to acquire some interests you did not have when you entered teaching. Take a few minutes of class time periodically to discuss something currently in the news. Mention a television show or a movie you have seen, a book you have read, a concert or play you have attended. Be willing to present your views for discussion (but not necessarily for student adoption) on social or political problems or school rules and policies. Attend some school activities and mention them in your classes. In sum, be an interested, interesting person. Your students will see you as a complete human being, a person of many interests, perhaps even a man for all seasons. Your having chosen purposely the subject you are teaching will inevitably exert an influence on your students.

(2) Another general principle of behavior for you to consider following is to begin using your students' interests as soon as you learn them. If one of your students is a cheerleader, you could do worse than mention in passing your knowledge of the position she is so proud of. It may even be possible for you to use an activity of one of your students as part of a classroom lesson. For example, a student's interest in stamp collecting and classifying may be useful in introducing the classification principles of your subject. (Learning the interests of your students is a part of the

over-all pattern of knowing them, a subject treated in the discussion in Chapter One.)

(3) A third important principle is to expect good work from your students and to let them know that you expect it. Many students have a way of accomplishing little more than they think is expected of them. It is wise to temper your idealism here, however; your expecting the best your students can achieve will not automatically guarantee that you get the best. If most of your students are working hard for you, then you are making your point. It is especially important to demand some effort from students of little ability. Too many teachers callously dismiss students in their "slow" classes with the self-fulfilling assertion "They can't do anything." They *can* do something and will, provided you make it clear that you expect them to perform as well as they can.

Expecting good work from your students is a two-way street. You must be equally willing to work hard. Just as success begets success, so also is laziness on your part likely to beget laziness on the part of your students. It makes sense, too, to let your students know that you are working at your teaching. Let them see the plans that you have made, the conscientious work you have done in grading their test papers, the efforts you make in helping counsel them. Don't become maudlin in this regard, however, or get querulous: occasional displays will suffice.

(4) An important aspect of your behavior as a teacher-motivator is the use of praise. Your method of responding to students' recitations, the comments you write on their papers, the remarks you make on their special projects can be of significant aid in your task of motivating students. A judicious use of praise is probably a better course here than is a showering of flattery all over the place. A little praise goes a long way; giving a student three stars every time he groans loudly is likely soon to dissipate the effectiveness of any praise you use. Discretion is clearly in order. However, when a student does something worth your compliments, extend them. He will be motivated to try again to earn your praise.

(5) Be frank with your students. Though this principle might seem one that could legitimately govern all aspects of your life, it can be especially important in motivating your students. If the class is not going as you would like it to go, your seeing a principal or department head or returning to books like this one for help will probably serve you less well than will an open discussion with the class. After all, your students are involved, too, and one can presume that they have similar hopes for a solution to the problem.

(6) Try to make your class an exciting place. Using a variety of instructional techniques is usually much better than an overreliance on one, no

matter how effective that one method sometimes is. Having a multi-activitied class in which several different activities (e.g., a short quiz, a recitation period, a study session) go on during one class period tends to keep the attention levels up. Use gimmicks occasionally, even games to maintain interest, for when students are interested they are likely to be motivated.

(7) It is good practice to let your students know what they are learning. Far too often teachers regard review as the students' job and never once mention what has been done in the class in previous lessons. Expressions like "Yesterday we discussed..." or "Last week you learned..." are good ways to alert your students that they are, in fact, learning.

(8) Finally, let your students know how you feel about teaching. Though this next prescription is blunt, I hope it will be followed: *If you don't like teaching, get out.* Just as one rotten apple is alleged to spoil the whole barrel, so also can one unhappy teacher ruin the whole day, each and every day, for his students, even though he may see them only one period. But if, as I more fervently hope, you do like teaching, let your students share your happiness and excitement.

In the intensity of your excitement, however, maintain some perspective. If the lesson goes badly one day, despair not, but pick up the pieces the next day and forge ahead. No one period is all that important. (If you doubt me on this point, ask yourself what went on in your own ninth grade English class on October 17.) Relax and enjoy your teaching. Acquire and retain a sense of humor. This posture of contentment can be infectious and from it your students can soon come to share your enthusiasm. Once they do, once they know they can approach your class with excited anticipation, any problems with motivation you might encounter will have largely solved themselves.

CLASSROOM PRESENTATIONS

Although the planning and motivation you do in preparation for a class are crucial to the success of that class, it is the actual on-stage performance that draws the critics' (your students') raves or boos. An effective presentation can, in fact, somewhat atone for rather hasty or ill-conceived planning or bad motivational preparation; conversely, a poor presentation can make worthless the best of plans and motivational techniques. It is appropriate, therefore, for you to give some attention to certain of the more common methods of presentation available to you in your teaching.

Lecture. The method of presentation with which you are probably most familiar is the lecture. As you well know from the many lectures you have attended in college, in this method the teacher speaks in a more or less formal manner to the total group for the entire period. He often speaks from notes and the expectation is that his students will take notes on what he says. Indeed, one wag once defined the lecture as a means of passing information from the notes of the teacher to the notes of his students without its going through the heads of either. If this describes the kind of lecturing you do, it will be prudent for you to discard this method of teaching.

Begun on this rather negative note about lecturing, let us continue with the bad points. First of all, the lecture tends to be overused in the secondary schools. This is quite understandable, as beginning teachers have just recently completed four years of training that were largely comprised of lectures. But the point remains that secondary school youth are not college students and to subject them to daily rounds of lectures is to demand more of their attention spans than they can deliver.

The lecture is also, even when well done, only passive learning at best; rare, indeed, is the lecturer who can excite more than a few of his students using only this method of presentation. More common is that lecturer whose students sit in various states of inattention, even of sleep, for long portions of the lecture. Many of these students take notes only because this activity keeps them awake. Even with the good lecturer before them, junior or senior high school students are less likely to respond to a lecture than to one of the methods presented below that give them a chance for active involvement.

A third caveat about lecturing of which you should be aware is that it is not easy. If you are going to lecture well, you are going to have to prepare thoroughly. Unlike in recitation lessons or in small group work, in lecturing you are the whole show and have only your preparation and glibness to rely on. You are center stage for the entire length of time of the lecture. Further, if the lecture is not going well, it is hard to shift gears into another activity.

But there is a positive side to lecturing, too. It is a very efficient means of transmitting information. It can be invaluable in explaining a process or presenting facts that you want your students to get in a certain relationship. The lecture can serve well to introduce units and to review what has been covered during them. It is more manageable than other kinds of instructional techniques, as only you are talking and, thus, you can control what is said. There is also some justification for your lecturing to those of your students who plan on going to college, as this will be the dominant method of their instruction once they get there. Finally, the lecture can be a good change of pace, both for you and for your students. Reluctant though I am to reveal the climax of the tale this early in the chapter, the culminating point of this section on teaching methods will be that a variety of instructional methods ought to be used in all secondary school classrooms; among them lecturing is deserving of a place.

Discussion/Recitation. Probably the most common method of instruction in the secondary schools is that in which both pupils and teachers talk. Whether this method merits the label "discussion" or "recitation" depends on the degree of teacher involvement. Quite often a teacher congratulates himself on having led a wonderful discussion when an observer of the period would have called the activity a recitation. If the talk is usually between one student and the teacher, with the other students tuning in or out according to their own desires, it is probably best considered a recitation period. First the teacher calls on Jane, who answers his question. The next question goes to Bob, who does not know the answer. Sally does, however, and raises her hand to recite. Bill next asks the teacher a question. In short, a recitation period is characterized by the teacher's being very much involved in the interchange.

A discussion implies less teacher involvement and more student participation. When Bill and Sally and Jane and Bob all talk—politely and with some degree of order, of course—without any more extensive teacher participation than his calling on the next to speak (and often without even this much direction), then the procedure is aptly called a discussion. In such an activity the focus is more on what the students say and less on what the teacher says, as is typically the case in recitation.

Interestingly, the need to maintain order in the classroom has resulted in practices which, when misused, further the incidence of recitation and lessen that of discussion. Chief among these is the practice students follow of raising their hands before they talk. The recognition the teacher makes of the raised hand puts him somewhat into the forefront of the discussion/recitation. If it is real discussion you want, it is wise to let politeness and courtesy control student talking, rather than your acknowledgment of the upraised hand. A second practice stems from the teacher's feeling that he must comment on each student's comment, however banal or vapid the student's remark may be. This procedure, too, involves the teacher more. For what it is worth I suggest that you try to avoid commenting after each student has spoken, reserving your remarks for those times when you really have a point to make. A third practice more conducive to recitation than to discussion is the typical classroom arrangement. Even with movable chairs most classrooms are still arranged with seats like the crosses in Flanders Field—row upon row. A student who must discuss his ideas with the back of another student's head may decide to forget all about it and shut up instead. Finally, there is the reluctance of some teachers ever to have a moment of quiet in the room while a discussion or recitation is under way. Such teachers seem to equate chatter with learning. Whenever there is a moment of silence, these teachers leap in to fill the void. Hence, more teacher involvement, more recitation, less discussion.

If you detected a bias in the foregoing remarks in favor of discussion, you read the passage well. A place in every classroom exists for recitation, to be sure, but not infrequently a classroom recitation is little more than a lecture occasionally interrupted by a teacher's question or a student's response. The good recitation, of which the Socratic dialogues serve as excellent examples, is one in which the student responders are being led toward certain outcomes by their teacher, who so phrases his questions that these outcomes may be reached. This kind of recitation period requires considerable planning. If you do not know in advance what you hope to accomplish in your recitation lesson, it may turn into a kind of "now . . . what?" session: "Now that I've asked this, what do I ask next?" It also requires something akin to a performer's stage presence, as you must develop the sensitivity to decide quickly when to stay with one question and when to shift to another one.

No less demanding is the discussion lesson, in which the teacher is much more a listener than in the recitation lesson. If you want to be a leader of good total-class discussion among secondary school students, you must develop a rather high tolerance for comments which are obvious, irrelevant, or absurd (or all three at once). That such comments will occur in the discussions you have in your classes ought in no way to deter you from having this kind of presentation. Students can learn much from such classroom activities, and not only about the subject they are discussing. They learn certain of the manners necessary if the discussion is to proceed fruitfully; they learn to express themselves in ways designed to influence or stimulate the thinking of others; they learn to listen. Indeed, these kinds of learning may eventually be more important than the seemingly more substantive ones which deal with the topics being discussed.

Total class discussion, with many of the students involved at some time during the discussion session, is enhanced if certain changes can be made in the typical classroom. A circle can replace the row-upon-row alignment of chairs and, thus, students can see each other when they talk. Having student leaders periodically helps; these leaders can even devise the questions that will start the discussion. Letting students respond without first raising their hands and being called on both permits freer discussion and teaches them something of discussion manners. This breaking away from traditional classroom practices and providing an atmosphere for open discussion can give you the opportunity to have really exciting classes.

Small Group Discussions. One rather commonly used type of discussion is the small group discussion, in which several students meet to discuss the topic of the lesson. If structured well, either by you or by your students, these can be beneficial lessons; if unstructured, they are likely to degenerate into student gossip groups about the upcoming dance or the latest dating twosome. If you intend using small groups extensively, you should probably vary the methods by which you select the members of the groups. Sometimes putting all the slow students in one group gives each the chance to succeed denied him when he is with brighter students. Mixing students of different abilities, with the added direction that the more able are to help the less able, can be effective. Putting all the shy students in a group almost forces at least one of them to come out of his shell; frequently all of them will.

Your behavior while the groups are meeting can be crucial to their success. It is not the time for you to sit at your desk and grade papers or catch a needed nap. Rather, if you circulate among the groups, pausing here and there to add a comment or answer a question, you can soon discover that this method of small group discussion is another valuable tactic in your repertory of teaching strategies.

Independent Study. The final method to be examined in this brief overview of teaching methods is that of independent study. Sometimes called the project or laboratory approach, this teaching strategy calls for a student's working on his own, either at a task given him by his teacher or one he has selected for himself. Whether you single out one student and have him do something different from what the others are doing or have the entire class work on independent study projects, you will soon discover that much of the success of this independent work lies in its design. If the individual student has a clear direction for his project and a planned evaluation of his work, good results can follow; if he is just to "go do something," the results may not be impressive.

The lecture, the recitation, the discussion (total class or small group), the individual assignment—these are some but by no means all of the instructional techniques available to you. With some of them you will achieve your goals better than with others, but it is good practice to try a variety of techniques. There is no one royal road to teaching success; you should try several different teaching tactics to discover your effectiveness with each. It is wise, too, to vary the techniques you employ during each period. Such multi-activitied lessons can be stimulating and can provide the kinds of results that make all your planning and motivation worthwhile.

FOR FURTHER READING

Bellock, Arno A., "What Knowledge Is of Most Worth?" *The High School Journal*, 48, Feb. 1965, 318-22.

Bent, Rudyard K., and Adolph Unruh, *Secondary School Curriculum*, Chap. 3. Lexington, Mass.: D. C. Heath and Company, 1969.

Besvinick, Sidney L., "An Effective Daily Lesson Plan," *The Clearing House*, 34, Mar. 1960, 431-33.

Bloom, Benjamin, ed., *Taxonomy of Educational Objectives, Handbook I: Cognitive Domain.* New York: Longmans, Green and Company, 1956.

Douglas, Leonard M., *The Secondary Teacher at Work*, Chaps. 11 and 12. Boston: D. C. Heath and Company, 1967.

Esbensen, Thorwald, "Writing Instructional Objectives," *Phi Delta Kappan*, 48, Jan. 1967, 246-47.

Hoover, Kenneth H., *Learning and Teaching in the Secondary School*, Chaps. 3, 4, and 5. Boston: Allyn and Bacon, Inc., 1964.

Inlow, Gail M., *Maturity in High School Teaching*, Chaps. 4 and 5. Englewood Cliffs, N.J.: Prentice-Hall, Inc., 1963.

Krathwohl, David R., Benjamin S. Bloom, and B. B. Masia, *Taxonomy of Educational Objectives, Handbook II: Affective Domain. New York:* David McKay Company, Inc., 1964.

Riessman, Frank, "Some Suggestions for Teaching the Culturally Deprived," *NEA Journal*, 52, Apr. 1963, 20-22.

Sanders, Norris M., *Classroom Questions: What Kinds?* New York: Harper & Row, Publishers, 1966.

Taba, Hilda, and Deborah Elkins, *Teaching Strategies for the Culturally Disadvantaged*, Chaps. 3-11. Chicago: Rand McNally and Company, 1966.

Trump, J. Lloyd, and Delmas F. Miller, *Secondary School Curriculum Improvement*, Chaps. 18, 19, and 20. Boston: Allyn and Bacon, Inc., 1968.

CHAPTER THREE

The Teacher
and
Discipline

THE RETORT DISCOURTEOUS

In your remedial reading class you purposely have tried to create an informal atmosphere, believing that your students can improve in reading only if they are relaxed and feel secure. You often begin the period with a general discussion of some topic you think the students will be interested in and permit them to talk freely about it. This procedure, you think, has added much to your success with these students.

Just now, however, you had cause to wonder about your methods. Susan, perhaps the least able and the least popular student in your class, was giving her opinion of a school rule on smoking in the restrooms. Right in the middle of her discourse, Bill yelled from across the room, "That's not true, you stupid idiot."

"It is too true, you dirty————," retorted Susan. "You're nothing but a dumb————." Susan's specific and detailed remarks about Bill's legitimacy and his mother implied that Susan needed some help with vocabulary as well as reading. They also rendered the rest of your class mute as they waited expectantly for you to act.

What are you going to do? Susan's vulgarity deserves some punishment, yet she did have some provocation from Bill's interruption. Too, you think, the informality of the class may lead on occasion to such volatility. Perhaps you should simply murmur something about the incident and let it pass.

Meanwhile, your class is still waiting.

YOUR SOLUTION

YOUR REACTIONS TO THE ALTERNATE SOLUTIONS

ALTERNATE SOLUTIONS

1. Send both Bill and Susan to the school disciplinarian and let him handle the problem.

2. Ask Bill and Susan to come to your room after school and talk to them both, especially to Bill about interruptions and to Susan about her less-than-ladylike language.

3. Right after the incident demand that each apologize to the other and then launch into a discussion of (a) appropriate procedures of classroom discussion and (b) profanity.

4. Quietly treat the whole incident as though it had not happened. Ask Susan to continue her discussion of what she thinks of the smoking rule.

5. Say that the discussion period is closed for the day and that, if similar eruptions occur in the future, you will do away with the discussion sessions. Proceed with your planned lesson.

CHAOS 101

You recall with something less than humor how one of your college professors laughingly had told you that study halls were passé, that schools nowadays rarely used them. Those schools that still did have study halls, he added, usually employed teachers' aides to run them. How wrong he was! In fact, you'd be most happy if he would come to your school and take over your study hall, which you have privately labeled "Chaos 101."

The first few days went smoothly enough. There was some talking among a few students who apparently had very little studying that they wanted to do. Occasionally a spitball would fly across the room and once even a chalkboard eraser became airborne. These acts, though, were individual ones, ones you could handle by reprimanding the one or two students involved.

Your success with these individual cases did not prepare you well for the concerted group efforts which succeeded them. For seven straight days now there has been, at least once each session, a group disruption that involved over two-thirds of the class. One day the students all coughed loudly at 10:15 and again at 10:25, the second occurrence coming just after the laughter which had followed the first had subsided. The next day most of the students slid their heaviest books off their desks at an obviously prearranged time. Another time practically all of the students crumpled papers and began walking with them to the wastebasket.

Yesterday, however, was the worst. At 10:20 most of the students dropped a handful of marbles on the floor and then laughed as the marbles went pinging and zinging their way around the room. Your insisting that the students pick up the marbles wasn't exactly wise either, as the students seemed only too eager to leave their seats for this unplanned (by you, at least) exercise. You had only a wan smile of sympathy for the student who remarked to you on her way out of the study hall, "I need the time in here to study. Why don't you control the situation?"

Yes, you think, why don't you? But how?

YOUR SOLUTION

YOUR REACTIONS TO THE ALTERNATE SOLUTIONS

ALTERNATE SOLUTIONS

1. Keep the entire study hall after school, knowing full well that such a punishment is unfair to the one-third who have not participated in the group shenanigans.

2. Go to the school disciplinarian with the matter and tell him of the problem. Demand that you be given help.

3. Try to use those who want the time to study to ferret out the ring-leaders. Once you discover them, punish them very severely.

4. Have an open discussion in the study hall about the kind of study hall the students want to have.

5. Appoint student officers of the study hall whose job it is to keep disruptions to a minimum and to inform you of the leaders in any group action.

6. The next time something happens, join in the fun. If marbles are thrown, pick some up and throw them. If all cough, you cough, too. Let the students see that you are a good sport about it all and then perhaps you can launch into your talk about appropriate study hall behavior.

"MARCIA'S ABSENT AGAIN!"

You've about had it with Marcia. She is again absent on the day of your biology test. You have given three tests already this year and Marcia has been absent each time. In each instance, however, she appeared the next day, fully recovered, with an excuse approved by the people in the attendance office. Their approval, you know, is contingent upon Marcia's presenting a signed note from her mother explaining the cause of her absence. The notes are not forgeries. You suspect that Marcia's mother is either being fooled or is participating in the plot. There is also the possibility that Marcia becomes genuinely sick on the day of your tests, but you rather doubt that this is so, especially since today you overheard one student say to another, "Biology test and Marcia's absent again. It figures."

After her first absence you gave Marcia the same questions the next day, sending her to the library during class time to take the test. She wrote an excellent paper. The second time you made her come in after school and make up the test and again she did very well. As your tests are composed of short essay questions, the kind which are easy to pass on from one student to another, you suspect that Marcia had sought and received information about the tests from her fellow students who had taken it at the assigned time. The third time, therefore, you wrote an entirely different test, a most time-consuming and laborious process. Marcia did poorly on the test, confirming your suspicions. You know, however, that you do not have the time to make out duplicate tests and have resolved, therefore, to deal effectively with Marcia the next time she misses a test.

Well, that next time has come. What are you going to do?

YOUR SOLUTION

YOUR REACTIONS TO THE ALTERNATE SOLUTIONS

ALTERNATE SOLUTIONS

1. Tell Marcia that, starting with this test, you are not going to permit her to make up any more tests she misses. Her grade will be based on only the work she does at the proper time.

2. Assign a difficult essay for Marcia to write for every test she misses and grade it very stringently, hoping that she will come to understand that it is in her best interests to take the tests with the rest of the class.

3. Call Marcia's mother and discuss the problem with her, telling her that you *just know* that she does not realize that Marcia is missing tests when she is absent.

4. Tell Marcia that, on future tests she misses, you will require a doctor's confirmation of her illness before you will permit her to make up the work.

5. Discuss openly with the class, with Marcia out of the room on some pretext, what you should do.

6. Change your testing to include many objective items that cannot be easily passed along by the other students in the class.

7. Talk with Marcia, telling her of your suspicions and asking her to change her ways.

THIS CULOTTE BUSINESS

One of the rules at the school at which you are a first year teacher is that the school dress code must be enforced to the letter by all teachers. Fresh from college, where any and all dress styles were allowed, you question a bit whether the rule against short skirts and culottes is realistic but decide that, if you are faced with enforcing it or not, you will go along with the school policy. Today, though, when you discovered that Janet in your first period class was wearing culottes, you wondered whether you should send her to the office where she would be given a lecture by the dean and an automatic three-day suspension.

Janet is, you think, a special case, deserving of extra consideration. She is not a good student, but she tries and has lately been showing more interest in school, or at least more interest in your bookkeeping class. You have heard, too, that her home life is pretty sordid and think it unwise to give her an enforced vacation of three days.

After class, therefore, you spoke to Janet, telling her that you weren't going to turn her in because of the culottes, but that she should not wear them again. She became irate and argued that her culottes were both neater and longer than the skirts worn by some of the "rich kids." You had to agree. She went on, "It's a stupid rule. Why shouldn't I be allowed to wear what I want?"

Finally, you were able to calm Janet down and convince her that, though she might think the rule stupid and maybe it was a bit silly, it was still a rule to be obeyed and enforced. More rational now, she agreed that she would not again wear clothes that violated school policy.

At lunch Mr. Collins, who is considered by the students to be the most rigid teacher in the school, approached you and told how he had sent Janet to the office for wearing culottes when she came to his second period class. "Furthermore," he went on, "I told the principal that you had said to Janet that the dress policy was silly. You new teachers must come to understand that we have to have these rules and enforce them or we'll have anarchy."

On your way back to class you stopped for your mail and discovered a note from the principal, requesting that you have a conference with him about "this culotte business."

What are you going to tell him?

YOUR SOLUTION

YOUR REACTIONS TO THE ALTERNATE SOLUTIONS

ALTERNATE SOLUTIONS

1. Be abject in your apology and tell the principal that, henceforth, you will rigidly enforce the school rules.

2. Explain the "whys" of your making an exception in Janet's case and urge that she not be suspended.

3. Tell him that you're going to take the whole incident to other faculty members and solicit their opinions both of your behavior regarding Janet's culottes and of Mr. Collin's behavior regarding you, a fellow teacher.

4. Urge the principal to establish a student-faculty committee to reconsider the school dress code to establish whether it is realistic and enforceable. Offer your services as chairman if he wants them.

DISCIPLINE

If the thesis developed in the prefatory note of this text is accurate—if, that is, teachers leave teaching or are unhappy or unsuccessful while teaching because of problems related to concerns other than those of their subject matter—then one must attend to these concerns. Among them discipline ranks high. It is not easy to manage a class of exciting and excitable adolescents whose interests are seemingly as boundless as the energies with which they pursue them. They talk, they squirm, they fight, they throw things, they even listen occasionally; in short, they behave in about the same ways you and your friends behaved when you were their age.

Somehow you survived and so did most of your teachers. This survival, especially of your teachers, suggests that the problems that students cause can be dealt with, if not always as effectively as one would like, then at least satisfactorily enough to permit the educational show to continue. But the survival may be that much easier, the solutions that much closer to perfection if you have a few basic understandings about discipline in the schools.

New and relatively inexperienced teachers are often told that they need only have exciting and interesting classroom lessons and they will have no discipline problems. As with much often-repeated advice, there is a kernel of truth in this statement, but it is certainly not the all-encompassing pronouncement some of its proponents seem to believe it to be. Consider the case of Johnny, who is caught cheating and subsequently embarrassed in the class he has before coming to yours. During the passing period he is rebuffed by his girl friend. Attempting to get to your class on time, he is stopped by the principal for running in the hall and issued a one-hour detention. By the time he gets to your class he is ready to explode, and your lesson, even if it is one that would do credit to a Socrates, Pestalozzi, and John Dewey, may not deter that explosion. You, then, are confronted both with a discipline problem and with some doubts about the wisdom of those who told you that an interesting class, like love, conquers all.

Still, though, the best defense against an outbreak of discipline problems is the good lesson. (See Chapter Two.) When students are excited about what they are doing, about the kinds of activities you have them involved in, about what they are learning, they are less likely to be disruptive of the class proceedings.

Another difficulty that arises with any discussion of discipline is that of definition. What may be an orderly classroom for one teacher is thought of as chaos by another. Gum chewing, for example, is viewed by some teachers as permissible behavior; others regard it as a serious disciplinary infraction. The best, probably, that can be said is that matters of discipline, like many other aspects of teaching, are highly individualized, depending primarily on how you, the teacher, regard them. In developing a position, you will perforce attend to factors that vary from class to class: the number of students, their age and ability levels, their interest (or lack of it) in the subject you teach, etc. Many psychologists contend that even the atmospheric pressure has a significant bearing on the restlessness of students.

Despite these differences there are some generalizations one can make about discipline. In general parlance the word "discipline" has to do with control, usually a control that is self-imposed. So is it in education, in which discipline is regarded as classroom control; indeed, "discipline" and "classroom management" are often used interchangeably. Control of the classroom, then, is what you must strive to maintain, but it is a control, or management, that you can tailor to your purposes. If, for instance, you think your class is most efficiently run—if, that is, your students learn best—in an informal situation, then that is the kind of classroom climate you should endeavor to create. If you think a greater degree of formality is necessary, then work toward that end.

Your means of effecting the kind of classroom you want will vary, but some general principles apply. The fewer the rules you have for the maintenance of an effective learning environment, the better off you are likely to be. The code by which some students live seems to be that "rules are made to be broken"; your creating a massive list of "Thou shalt's" and "Thou shalt not's" may serve to spark disciplinary problems that would never occur without the rules and the attendant desire of some students to try to break them and get away with something.

But be consistent. Those rules you do make, you have every right to enforce. To bark at a student for talking one day and then to ignore the same misbehavior the next day is to risk having none of your rules obeyed. Consistent enforcement, though, is only one side of the coin; the other is consistent punishment. Though you can expect some disciplinary cases that you must treat as individual, generally a safer course is to punish one student for one misdeed exactly the same way you would punish another student for the same misdeed.

The punishment for infractions is really another topic altogether and texts are filled with suggestions for you to follow. Many of these deal with punishments you are already familiar with from your own high school days: changing seating patterns to prevent, or make more difficult, classroom conversations; issuing detention slips requiring the student to stay after school a specified time; conferring individually with the student; even spanking a student, though this last example, a carry-over from the days when corporal punishment was common in schools, is much less in vogue today.

Whatever punishment you do mete out should be accompanied, I believe, by a certain mental attitude on your part. First of all, if you can minimize the outbreak of the discipline problem and continue with the lesson, you are well advised to do so. That teacher who stops the entire class to tongue lash a couple of students who are mildly disruptive may himself create more problems than if he were to let the students talk. Often just a simple "See me after class" to the offenders can quiet them and, at the same time, permit you the short conference at the end of the period when you can berate them as much as you wish. More importantly, it does not break into the classroom activity.

A second, and vastly more significant, part of the attitude you take toward punishment is that your punishment ought to be directed more toward correcting future behavior than toward punishing past behavior. The outbreak, the talking, the throwing of chalk, whatever occurred to cause you to want to punish someone is past history; what you need to be more concerned about is the future performance of these students who are misbehaving. Indeed, sometimes your thinking of the future behavior and, thus, letting a fractious student get off the hook can be more beneficial than will a severe reprimand or an embarrassing scene. Little but a deserved resentment from your students will result from your letting punishment become retaliation; you need constantly to keep in mind that you and your offending students will be together again tomorrow and the next day and the one after that. It is, therefore, a self-serving wisdom to consider your disciplinary measures as a means of improving future behavior.

Occasionally, however, you must punish—and punish harshly. Yours will be a rare teaching career if you never once really lose your temper at a student and do or say something which, on later, calmer reflection, both annoys and embarrasses you. In some of these instances the student who provoked your loss of self-control well deserves all you can hand out; punish him and be done with it. In others he may not deserve quite the wrath you direct his way. When these latter occurrences take place, and be assured that they will, they are best forgotten as soon as possible. Sometimes you may need to placate a student whom you punished overmuch, but do keep in mind that teenagers are resilient; the student will doubtlessly suffer far less than you think.

Finally, no discussion of discipline can be regarded as complete without some attention to your position as disciplinarian vis-a-vis that of the principal or dean of the school. Some principals quite openly expect their teachers to handle all but the most flagrant violations of school or classroom policy and, in so doing, manage to convey the impression that they do not want any students at all sent to them for punishment. Most principals, however, are very willing to help out, especially with severe problems. Quite busy with the many tasks of administering a school, they naturally do not want to deal with the occasional chatterbox or with the student whose only sin is that he has once more failed to bring a pencil to class. But on the more serious cases—open insubordination, fighting, excessive classroom disruptions, and the like—they are eager to take corrective measures. If you have a problem that you believe is beyond your ability to handle or would take too much time from the other students, let the principal know. Try to handle the discipline problems yourself, but do remember that you have as resources capable people who probably once taught themselves and will be both sympathetic and helpful.

The proof of the wisdom of the foregoing brief remarks on discipline is, of course, subject to classroom testing. It does seem, though, that the generalizations suggested above—that a good lesson can work wonders with even the most unruly class, that your use of punishment should be directed toward improving future behavior, that the principal can be an effective person to turn to when real trouble strikes—are supported by thousands of teachers for whom discipline is a problem encountered more in books like this one than in their classrooms.

FOR FURTHER READING

Ausubel, David, "A New Look at Classroom Discipline," *Phi Delta Kappan,* Oct. 1961, 25-30.

Batchelder, Henry H., "Corrective Measures, Punishment, and Discipline," *Journal of Secondary Education,* 39, Feb. 1964, 86-93.

Clark, Leonard H., and Irving S. Starr, *Secondary School Teaching Methods* (2nd ed.), Chap. 4. New York: The Macmillan Company, 1967.

Hall, Nason E., "Saving the Trouble Prone," *NEA Journal,* 49, Apr. 1965, 24-29.

Hand, Harold C., *Principles of Public Secondary Education,* Chap. 7. New York: Harcourt, Brace & World, Inc., 1958.

Hymes, James L., *Behavior and Misbehavior.* Englewood Cliffs, N. J.: Prentice-Hall, Inc., 1955.

Inlow, Gail M., *Maturity in High School Teaching,* Chap. 15. Englewood Cliffs, N. J.: Prentice-Hall, Inc., 1963.

Oliva, Peter F., *The Secondary School Today,* Chaps. 16, 17, 18. New York: The World Publishing Company, 1967.

CHAPTER FOUR

The Teacher and Evaluation

LOST, STRAYED, OR STOLEN: ONE GRADE BOOK

Just two weeks before the end of the marking period, you discover that your grade book is missing. You believe that it was taken from your classroom, perhaps by one of your students, but, for whatever reason it has disappeared, you no longer have the many grades you had recorded for the 139 students in your Spanish classes. What disappoints you even more is that you believe you had done a good job on the grading for a beginning teacher; you had several major test grades, some homework grades, and even some marks on individual recitation and daily work. You had thought that you would be able to make an objective and thorough evaluation of the work of each student during this marking period.

When you tell them of your loss, both your department head and your principal begin a search, but with no success.

Your problem, however, is less the missing grade book and more what you are going to do with the approaching date for turning in term grades. What are you going to do?

YOUR SOLUTION

YOUR REACTIONS TO THE ALTERNATE SOLUTIONS

ALTERNATE SOLUTIONS

1. Give each student one or two tests and let the grades on these determine the grades for the entire marking period.

2. Rely on memory and do the best job you can.

3. Ask each student to estimate on a sheet of paper the grade he thinks he deserves for the marking period. Assume that each student will be honest and give him the grade he believes he should get.

4. Tell the students what happened, enlisting their help in searching for the grade book. If it is not found, ask the students to recall as many of their grades as they can.

ANYONE FOR TRUE-FALSE?

The first test of your brand new career of teaching high school economics has been a complete disaster. And yet, prior to giving it, you believed the test had merit. You gave five essay questions on which you thought your seniors, many of them very bright, would be able to display well what they had learned.

You first sensed the trouble when students began complaining about the length of the test while they were taking it. Two or three told you afterwards that it was the first essay test they had ever taken and they had not managed their time well. Yet two students had finished the test completely and had done fairly good, if somewhat superficial, work.

But there were other problems. Betsy, for example, had written answers to only two of the five questions, but these two answers were superb indeed, by far the best in the class on those two questions. Bruce had obviously spent so long in preparing his good answer to question No. 1 that he had had to rush through the other four questions and had not revealed what you are certain he knows. Kathy had skipped question No. 1 entirely, had written only a short paragraph on question No. 2, but had done the rest rather thoroughly and rather well. Barbara, the one student who had turned in her paper before the bell, had answered the first question and then had written a note: "I have read the other questions and think I know how to answer them, but I don't have the time. I know I'm going to flunk anyway, so what's the use? Your test was just plain too long."

Yes, your test was just plain too long. But what are you going to do about it?

YOUR SOLUTION

YOUR REACTIONS TO THE ALTERNATE SOLUTIONS

ALTERNATE SOLUTIONS

1. Scrap the whole test as a bad job and forget that you ever gave it.
2. Give the examination again, this time as a take-home test over an extended period of time. Put your students on their honor not to seek outside help and hope that most of them will be honest.
3. Grade the papers as you had intended, equal credit for each question, even if this means that many of your students will fail because they did not complete the exam.
4. Ask your class what they want to do about the test, presenting them with some alternatives. Abide by the majority decision.
5. Grade what each student wrote as though that had been all that was required of him, even though this procedure might penalize those who answered most of the questions but did so superficially.

PAM'S MISSING PAPER

At the end of their period in the laboratory, you told your chemistry students to write their lab reports outside class and turn them in to you the next day. It was not until several days later that you began evaluating them and discovered that you did not have a paper from Pam. You concluded that she had not done the assignment and gave her a zero. Also you were not too surprised because, although Pam had always done her work before, she had not impressed you with her seriousness in school and often seemed to be doing just enough to get by.

At the conclusion of the class in which you returned the papers, Pam approached you and asked why hers had not been returned. You told her that she had not handed in a paper. Quietly but very adamantly, with a kind of cool aplomb you had to admire, Pam insisted that she had turned in a paper, placing it in your "in" tray with those of the rest of the class. You momentarily gave her the benefit of the doubt and said you would look for her lab report.

You made that search and did not find Pam's paper. Though you are skeptical of the truth of Pam's story, you are reluctant to assert positively that she is lying; it is possible that you did lose the paper.

It has now been almost two weeks since the day of the experiment. Thus, if you were to have Pam redo her written work, she could hardly be expected to remember her data. Moreover, she claims that she discarded the notes which she made during the lab period. To have her redo the entire experiment would cause problems, too, because most of the necessary materials have been put back into the storeroom. Yet you do not care to ignore wholly the assignment because, if Pam is lying, as you believe she is, she would be getting away with something; on the other hand, if she is telling the truth, making her redo the experiment would be punishing her for a mistake you made.

You finally decide to ignore the whole thing. When you tell Pam that you are going to erase the "0" and simply not average that work with her other work, she complains, saying that she had done a particularly good job on that assignment and that it surely would have been an "A" or "B" paper. Pam pleads that you are being unfair.

What are you going to do?

YOUR SOLUTION

YOUR REACTIONS TO THE ALTERNATE SOLUTIONS

ALTERNATE SOLUTIONS

1. Stick to your guns. Tell Pam that you are sorry, but that your decision about not including that one assignment in her average must be the final word on the subject.

2. Even though it means going to the storeroom and getting the lab materials, call Pam's bluff, tell her that you're sorry you lost her paper and also sorry that she must make up the work, and usher her into the lab. You might even tell her that, since she had done so well on the assignment, this second time around will cause her little trouble.

3. Give Pam credit for telling the truth and try to effect a compromise at a "B plus."

4. Tell Pam that you will not count the missing assignment, but will instead give her double credit for the next lab exercise. If she does well, she can get two good grades. If she does poorly, however, she will get two poor grades.

SAVED BY THE BELL

Right in the middle of your test in geometry the fire alarm sounded. School policy demands that students get out of the building as quickly as possible and your students seemed even more dutiful today than usual.

Though you watched carefully to see that no student smuggled a copy of the test out of the room, there was simply no way for you to keep the students from talking. And you're reasonably certain that your test was the number one topic of conversation.

It was almost ten minutes before the students returned to their desks. Time, you thought, might become a factor for the students but of greater concern to you was the amount of information that had changed hands while the students were out of the building.

And apparently some did: the class average was almost ten points higher than on previous tests. You had felt that you had done a better job of teaching prior to this test and that the scores might naturally be higher, but now, with the ten-minute unplanned chat in the middle of the test, you wonder.

Should you handle the grading any differently?

YOUR SOLUTION

YOUR REACTIONS TO THE ALTERNATE SOLUTIONS

ALTERNATE SOLUTIONS

1. Grade the tests as though the interruption had not occurred.
2. Use a much more difficult curve than usual, explaining to the class that information must have leaked out during the time the students were out of the room.
3. Evaluate the test as an aid to the learning of your students, but do not record the grades.
4. Subtract five points (splitting the difference in their usual averages and the scores on this test) and use your normal grading procedures.
5. Ask the students if they think you should make any changes and abide by their decision.

TO ERR IS HUMAN, BUT THIS IS RIDICULOUS

Having completed your third week of teaching world history in this, your first year of teaching, you have just given your first test, a 100-item multiple-choice exam that you knew was difficult but also felt was fair to your sophmores and juniors who are grouped in an "above average" section. Before the test you announced that you would use what you called a "college grading scale" of 100-90, "A"; 89-80, "B"; 79-70, "C"; 69-60, "D"; below 60, "F," feeling that this scale would permit most of the class to get fairly good grades and, thus, to begin the year confidently.

But tonight, as you graded the papers, your shock has been severe. The highest grade in the class is a 73; there are six scores in the 60's; the other twenty scores are all below 60—or failing according to the scale you announced to your class.

You realize that you are going to have to take some thoughtful stock of your teaching and testing practices. But that's not your immediate problem. You told your class that you would be returning their papers tomorrow. What concerns you is what grades you should put on the tests. You even have the not-so-fleeting thought that it might be wisest to throw the test away and forget that it ever happened.

What are you going to do?

YOUR SOLUTION

YOUR REACTIONS TO THE ALTERNATE SOLUTIONS

ALTERNATE SOLUTIONS

1. Grade the test just as you announced you would, even though twenty of the students fail.

2. Curve the scores in such a way that only the bottom few students fail, but announce to your class that this procedure will not be followed on future tests when the class does poorly.

3. Throw the tests away and tell the students that their scores were so low that you don't even want to return the tests.

4. Without returning the test, conduct a careful review and give the same test again. Average the two scores each student made and use the original grading scale.

5. Return the tests, scored but without any letter grades. Solicit the suggestions of your students about how you should handle the letter grades.

6. Add 27 points (the difference between the top score and 100) to each test and use the scale you originally announced.

SECOND TIME AROUND

As a first-year English teacher you have discovered that the grading of student writing is one of your biggest problems. Not only does it take an inordinate amount of time, but also you find yourself constantly wondering if you are grading the themes fairly and consistently. You pride yourself, though, that you are at least trying and are also willing to discuss your grading with your students.

You are not, however, prepared for the conversation with Jeff, one of your eleventh-graders. Questioning why he received a "C-" on one of his themes, he seems wholly unwilling to accept your explanation. Finally he tells you why he is angry. The paper he is complaining about is an exact copy of a theme he had submitted last year to Mr. Abbot, one of the old-time members of the English department; Mr. Abbot had given the paper a mark of "A." Further, he says that he has just come from Mr. Abbot who told him (Jeff says) that, despite your "C-" on it, he thought the paper still deserved an "A."

You're rather taken aback by Jeff's admission, but realize that a display of anger will get you nowhere. Your telling Jeff that your standards of evaluation may be different from Mr. Abbot's does not mollify him. Nor does your shifting gears into a discussion of the honesty of using an old paper. At last you are able to conclude the conference with Jeff by saying that you will take another look at his paper, but that you doubt that the reexamination will result in any change. And Jeff sullenly leaves.

You must decide what to do. Jeff's paper now does seem to have a little more merit than when you first read it, but hardly enough for a significantly higher grade. Moreover, you wonder what, if anything, you ought to do about Mr. Abbot's part in this whole business.

What are you going to do?

YOUR SOLUTION

YOUR REACTIONS TO THE ALTERNATE SOLUTIONS

ALTERNATE SOLUTIONS

1. Tell Jeff that the "C- " stands and that you are disappointed that he would use a paper he had written for another teacher. Say nothing about the incident to Mr. Abbot.

2. Raise Jeff's grade to "B-," but tell him that, from now on, you want this year's work. Talk with Mr. Abbot in a tactful way about the situation, but let him know that you think he acted unwisely.

3. Turn Jeff into the school disciplinarian for cheating and tell Mr. Abbot what you have done. Tell him, too, that you feel that he must bear some of the responsibility for Jeff's present dilemma and his earlier surliness about the grade he received.

4. Tell Jeff you are going to let him write another theme, the grade on which will replace the "C-" he was angry about. Tell Mr. Abbot that you would appreciate his not undermining your authority.

5. Go over the paper with Mr. Abbot. Let him show you why he thinks it is an "A" paper while you defend your choice of the "C-." Eventually give Jeff the compromise grade you and Mr. Abbot decide on.

6. Take the whole case to the department head or principal and follow his advice with respect both to Jeff's grade and to Mr. Abbot.

EVALUATION

Though evaluation of his students is a regular, ongoing part of a teacher's responsibility, it is a difficult task that, unlike many of the other problems in teaching, does not get easier the longer one teaches. Indeed, teachers of a number of years of experience now know more about grading and about students than they did as beginners, but, given this greater awareness, they often feel even more unsure of themselves in their work in evaluating student performance and growth. To be sure, they are inured to the complaints students are likely to make and have perfected techniques for handling some of the problems that plague new or relatively inexperienced teachers. But they also now understand that evaluation is, at its best, an inexact science, one governed by a variety of forces, not all of which are in the teacher's control.

One of the less obvious problems, for example, is that evaluation as a technique for improving instruction is required, in almost all secondary schools, to adhere to time alignments. Grades must be given every six or nine weeks and again at the end of the semester. Not infrequently, these are not the times a teacher would choose if he were given freedom to evaluate when he wanted to. The administrative imperative to issue all the grade reports at one time is obvious enough and will not be discussed here; suffice it to say that many thousands of tests are given each year, not because students need the tests at that time, but rather because teachers need one more grade for the marking period. In many of these instances, of course, the unit must be foreshortened, the enrichment activities set aside, the special projects dropped to make time for the test.

A second problem in grading is that it reduces to one mark or symbol an entire period of work and, thus, compounds even more the difficulties stressed elsewhere in this book that grades are all-important to students. And not only do these grades offer indications, however indefinite, about past work; they also influence future performance. After Johnny has worked hard for the "B" he thought he should get in math, his getting a "C" may well dampen his future willingness to work. In such a situation he pays little attention to what he has learned, to the facts, skills, and attitudes he has acquired; the grade is all.

These and other difficulties notwithstanding, and despite the valiant efforts of a few schools to do away with grades entirely, such marks are likely to be with us for a long time to come and to continue to be the major component of the evaluation made of a student. It will be to your advantage, therefore, to attend to some of the different philosophies about grading which teachers implement in their classrooms. Four such philosophies are presented below.

The first of the positions that commonly underlie grading systems is the belief that a grade should represent a student's achievement of the skills, abilities, and knowledges in a course as measured against an absolute standard decreed by the teacher or the department or even the school district. For example, a student can get an "A" in typing only if he meets the standard for an "A"; this standard might be that the student must type seventy words a minute with five or fewer errors in a five-minute typing test.

One of the implications of this philosophy bothers many teachers and causes some of them to slip away from this principle. Ranking students against a preset standard can mean that all students in a class can get the same grade, say all "B's" or all "F's." This situation would obtain if all have reached the same limit on the standards. If, to use the typing example given above, no student meets the "A" requirement, then no one receives an "A." This principle, then, carries with it the responsibility for a teacher to set standards that are realistic expectations for most of the students in a class.

Another philosophy which supports grading systems holds that the marks represent a student's achievement in a course measured against the achievements of his peers in the same course. The top score on a test, for example, earns an "A," the bottom score an "F." On such a basis grades will usually cover a full range, sometimes in the shape of the familiar bell curve, which has an approximately equal number of "A's" and "F's," larger and again roughly equal groups of "B's" and "D's," and a still larger group of "C's."

Although this principle of curving grades is probably followed by the majority of practicing teachers, it is not without its difficulties in application. Classes that are homogeneously grouped by school policy or by subject matter content (such as physics or Russian III) often have students who do not at all represent the normal school population; these students, if all are bright, may be penalized if their teacher chooses to use this philosophy in its extreme form: i.e., the bell curve. Some teachers are also reluctant to give students in lower-ability classes high grades, knowing that the academic level of their accomplishment is well below that of the least able student in the honors section. Other teachers, however, view a basic course in, say, English and an honors English course as two separate courses, just as chemistry and Spanish are two separate courses, and believe that the full range of grades can exist in both courses.

A third philosophy of grading involves the principle of measuring the student's work against some estimate of his ability. Thus, very good work indeed is required of the extremely able student if he is to receive a high grade. The slower student can earn a top grade with work that represents the best he can do, even though that work is innately inferior to that of his brighter classmates.

This position, like the others, has disadvantages at the level of practice. To be effective, it demands that a teacher make a very thorough diagnosis of the potential of each of his students. A simple pretest is not enough, as some students will purposely do poorly so that the demands on them will be less. Instead, the teacher must use as many tools of diagnosis as he has available—counselor records, test scores, recommendations of former teachers, even shrewd guesses—to measure the abilities of his students and, thus, to be in a position to assess what they can legitimately be expected to accomplish.

A fourth position on grading is one based on the relative progress of students. If Jimmy progresses more than Tommy, then Jimmy earns the higher grade. This practice, one often used in skills courses like physical education or shorthand, can be dangerous. If Jimmy and Tommy enter the course with similar abilities, then the measurement of the progress of the one against the progress of the other is essentially the same practice as that indicated in the second philosophy above. But if Jimmy far exceeds Tommy at the beginning of the course, there may be very little room for progress for him, whereas there is much for Tommy. Conceivably, under such a system, Tommy could double his skill and earn a higher grade than Jimmy, whose improvement was slight but whose skill is still much superior to Tommy's.

To these two latter positions is often added the element of effort. If a student seems to be making as much effort as can be expected of him, then he is rewarded, irrespective sometimes of any consideration of his achievement. Many fault this addition of effort as a criterion in evaluation, arguing that life rewards those who succeed, and not those who may try but do not succeed. Nonetheless, this examination of a student's effort does permit a teacher to hold out some chance for the hopelessly poor student who not only cannot succeed, he cannot even improve. With the use of effort as a grade determiner, if he tries, he passes.

What distresses many observers of the secondary schools is the way schools, departments, and even individual teachers shift from one philosophy to another, often unaware of any inconsistency. Some teachers, for example, openly pride themselves on giving the hardworking student a better grade, even at the same time the rest of their students are being graded on the absolute standard of achievement or on the classwide comparison of accomplishment. Worthy though their motives may be, one must still question the practices of these teachers and their failure to note their inconsistencies; certainly they are adding to the already too widespread confusion about grading. Emerson once argued that "A foolish consistency is the hobgoblin of little minds," but he wasn't teaching secondary school youth who are going to compare grades and wonder about inconsistencies, foolish or otherwise. There is indeed nothing at all foolish about consistency in grading, at least for a teacher, if not for a department or a school, as only such consistency can result in grades that are relatively meaningful in the same way for all—students, parents, guidance counselors, future employers, college admissions officers—who see them and interpret them.

What, finally, is the best advice for you? Very possibly, your wisest course is to choose that philosophy that seems to fit you and your subject most comfortably. Above all, whatever philosophy you choose, whether one of those presented above or another one entirely or even one demanded by the school in which you teach, try to be fair. That you really like Mary and would like to give her a higher grade should not, of itself, cause you to do so. Similarly, your dislike of Ellen ought not to justify your looking for ways to manifest that dislike on her report card.

In addition to consistency and fairness, openness with your students is worth striving for. Regardless of how you feel about grades, they are important to your students. Hence, the more you are willing to discuss openly and frankly how you are going to arrive at future grades or how you did arrive at past grades, the greater the chance of your escaping some of the problems associated with grading. Be willing to talk over an individual student's grade with him and, if he convinces you of your error, change his grade. It is, after all, his grade, not yours.

Try also to make your grades represent something in accord with the major purposes of your course. Far too many teachers grade upon a variety of assorted concerns like gum chewing or class behavior. If these are crucial matters in your class, then they appropriately deserve attention in your grading; if, as seems more likely, they are not that important, they should not be included in your arriving at an academic grade.

So far we have examined some statements of grading philosophy and the merits you will discover in being consistent, fair, and open. It is imperative also that we give some attention to the ways in which the grades are derived.

Examinations continue to be the most common device teachers employ to determine grades. Indeed, many teachers use test scores and nothing else. Such testing is usually of two types: objective and subjective. The former includes short-answer items such as true-false, multiple-choice, matching, or fill-in questions. The latter usually demands that a student write at some length in answer to a question or problem.

At the level of classroom practice both kinds of tests offer advantages and disadvantages. Time, always a factor to be considered in teaching, will often suggest which type of test you employ. The objective test, for example, requires the larger amount of time before it is given; this is, of course, the time required to make up the test. If you are wise, you will design this kind of test to facilitate your scoring it; using answer sheets or having all the answers on the left side of the page are useful techniques. The essay test, on the other hand, requires your time after it is given; you can make up the test comparatively quickly, but reading the answers is another matter.

The objective test can be marked consistently; the answer is usually either right or wrong. The essay test, though, permits considerable latitude in grading and often this grading includes, consciously or unconsciously, factors other than the content of the answer; writing facility and neatness are two examples of extrinsic factors that sometimes confound the problem of evaluating subjective tests.

The objective test, unless very skillfully designed, rarely permits much testing of attitudes and instead concentrates on knowledges and skills. The essay test can be prepared so that it forces a student to reveal his attitudes, though it, too, can call for a demonstration of facts and skills.

A significant advantage many teachers have found in objective tests is that the same one can be given to several different classes on the same day without much transmission of its content from class to class. If you have 150 multiple-choice questions, your students in the morning class are not likely to tell your students in the afternoon class too many of them over the lunch table. Information about an essay test, however, can and will travel fast, so fast, indeed, that your afternoon students may be writing their answers before you have even distributed the test.

Although the kind of test you use depends to a great degree on the subject you teach and the pupils you have, the existence of these pros and cons (by no means a complete list) suggests that you experiment with both. It also suggests that you ought not to rely entirely on tests in determining the grades your students are going to receive. To do so, in fact, may serve to lessen the usefulness of the tests as teaching devices, as your students may take them under such pressure that they are unable to give an accurate demonstration of what they have learned.

The kinds of testing discussed above are examples of full period tests, but tests of the same type can be given as short quizzes for ten or fifteen minutes. These quizzes can be useful in evaluation, too. Homework assignments, oral reports, participation in class discussions, special projects, all of these, if they are a part of your course, deserve consideration in your grading. Indeed, the more facets of your course you can include in your grading, the more satisfactory that grading is likely to be both for you and for your students.

But grading is only one of many aspects of evaluation, albeit the most important one and the most common one. Do try to communicate how you think your students are doing by means other than grades. Compliment a student on a job well done. Put outstanding work on the bulletin board. Try to schedule individual or group conferences periodically for the purpose of letting your students know how they stand. Keep the channels of communication sufficiently open so that a student can approach you at any time about his progress.

Try also to view the tools of evaluation you use, not as ends in themselves, but as means of effecting better learning for your students. You should allow time in your planning, for example, to go over a test, to reteach at that time what your students did not know and to reinforce what they did. You should try to explain to your class how you view the evaluation, how you see its place in the total picture of your teaching and their learning. In fact, if you can reach the point where you and your students agree on evaluation—the need for it, the methods used, the results obtained—many of the problems you may face in this vital area of education will solve themselves.

FOR FURTHER READING

Alexander, William M., "Reporting to Parents: Why? What? How?" *NEA Journal,* 48, Dec. 1959, 15-18.

Fensch, E. A., "Tone Down the Bell Curve," *The Clearing House,* 40, Apr. 1966, 468-71.

Gerberich, J. Raymond, Harry A. Greene, and A. N. Jorgensen, *Measurement and Evaluation in the Modern School.* New York: David McKay Company, Inc., 1962.

Husek, T. R., "Implications of Different Types of Evaluation for Test Development," *The High School Journal,* 51, Mar. 1968, 268-74.

Lien, Arnold J., *Measurement and Evaluation of Learning,* Chap. 5. Dubuque, Iowa: Wm. C. Brown Company, 1967.

McKean, Robert C., *Principles and Methods in Secondary Education,* Chap. 8. Columbus, Ohio: Charles E. Merrill Books, Inc., 1962.

Strang, Ruth, *How to Report Student Progress.* Chicago: Science Research Associates, 1955.

Thomas, R. M., *Judging Student Progress.* New York: Longmans, Green Company, 1960.

CHAPTER FIVE

The Teacher
and
Cheating

IN UNITY, THERE IS STRENGTH

Quite by chance, you discovered that Beth and Mary had turned in identical papers on your general science test. You remembered that the two girls had sat together at the same laboratory table while taking the exam, but you could not recall any evidence of copying. Still, the fact of cheating is irrefutable: both made a score of 81 on the 100 questions, both missed the same nineteen questions, and, as the clincher, both had put down the same incorrect answers on the ones they missed.

When you returned the tests, you wrote only "See me" on Beth's and Mary's papers. After class you spoke with them, showing them your evidence and saying that you felt that you had to give one or both of them "O's" for the test. You hoped, of course, that the guilty one would admit having cheated and that the problem could thus be solved without becoming too messy.

But each girl adamantly insisted that she hadn't copied. Nor did either accuse the other. Suspecting that perhaps their being together made each reluctant to tell the truth, you said you would remain in your room after school and invited either or both of the girls to see you individually. Your wish was that at least one of the girls would come in and either admit her own guilt or accuse the other.

It is now 4:30, one hour past the close of the school day, and neither girl has come to see you. What should you do next?

YOUR SOLUTION

YOUR REACTIONS TO THE ALTERNATE SOLUTIONS

ALTERNATE SOLUTIONS

1. Fail both girls. They obviously are in this thing together, with one doubtlessly helping the other and both agreeing to maintain their position of guiltlessness.

2. Ignore the cheating, give each girl the grade an 81 earned, and hope that their being caught, even if not punished, will cause them not to cheat in the future.

3. Insist that the two girls retake the test, this time separated and use the new test results to determine the cheater on the first one. Give the cheater "0," the other girl the "81."

4. Tell the two girls that, unless they are more open with you, you feel compelled to involve the principal or their parents or both in the problem.

5. See each girl separately, tell her that the other has accused her of cheating, and watch closely for her reactions as an indication of admitted guilt or maligned innocence.

AN AWARD-WINNING SHORT STORY—TWICE

As the teacher of the elective English offering in creative writing, you accepted the position of sponsor of the school literary magazine. The publication was fairly successful and earned you and the student writers, many of whom are in your creative writing class, considerable plaudits from your colleagues and superiors and even from the local newspaper.

Perhaps the best work in the magazine was Nancy's short story, one she had written for your class. When you suggested that she submit it to the magazine editorial board, she was reluctant. You attributed her holding back to modesty and persuaded her all the more; finally she agreed and the story was published. Nancy's entry won the "best story" award.

Today you wished that you had never seen Nancy's story. In your mailbox was an anonymous note which asserted that Nancy's story was "a direct copy" of a story which appeared in a college literary magazine some nine or ten years ago;" a copy of the college magazine is in our library." You checked and discovered that your informant was right on both counts: the magazine was in the library and Nancy's story was a verbatim copy. The original story had also won an award.

You really do not know what to do. Nancy is a senior due to graduate, with highest honors, in a few weeks. She is a member of the National Honor Society, whose code clearly proscribes the kind of plagiarism she is guilty of. If the copying were to become known, Nancy would be denied further participation in the group. Already Nancy has completed college plans and is going to a fine school on a full scholarship. Indeed, you recall checking "Unquestionably" on the question "Is the candidate honest?" on her recommendation form. The cheating she had done had earned her an "A" in your creative writing class, too. Nancy even wants to become a high school teacher of creative writing.

You can think of all sorts of pressures that may have caused Nancy to cheat when the short story assignment came due. But all that is past history. What are you going to do now?

YOUR SOLUTION

YOUR REACTIONS TO THE ALTERNATE SOLUTIONS

ALTERNATE SOLUTIONS

1. Confront Nancy with what you have discovered and ask her what she thinks you should do. A bright student, she may have some ideas for handling the situation.

2. Forget that you ever received the anonymous note and discovered the cheating.

3. Publish an apologetic explanation in the school newspaper and in the local newspaper, too, if it will accept it. In this note you can explain that the plagiarism went undetected until after the issue was published. Lower Nancy's grade sharply in the creative writing class. Let her know beforehand that you are going to do these things.

THE DISHONORED HONOR CODE

Having used the honor system during your college days, you were convinced that it would work in high school. Several of your teaching colleagues tried to persuade you otherwise, arguing that honor codes during examinations worked only when the entire educational institution employed them. You held a different view and debated that one class in one school—your geography class—could use the honor code effectively during a test.

When the members of your class seemed to agree with you, you secured permission to be gone from the room during the next test, to leave your students on their honors not to cheat. You explained the procedure to your ninth-graders and told them that they would have to sign the honor pledge: "I have neither given nor received aid on this examination."

The results were disastrous. You gave the same kind of test you have used all year, a 100-item objective exam involving true-false, multiple-choice, matching, and fill-in questions. Whereas on previous tests the class average had been around 78 or 80, on this test, if anything a harder one, the average was over 90. No one in the room scored below 80. Yet all of the students signed the honor code, though one student added, "But I sure did see plenty of aid given and received."

What is now your problem is what to do with the test. You know that many students were involved in the cheating, but believe that some were not. Punishing all by lowering all the grades is unfair to these people. Nor is throwing the test out an ideal solution, as it is a major grade for this marking period. Trying to discover the cheaters probably will not work; if they were willing to sign the honor pledge, surely they would deny cheating.

Meanwhile, you have to face your class and to decide what to do with the tests. What are you going to do?

YOUR SOLUTION

YOUR REACTIONS TO THE ALTERNATE SOLUTIONS

ALTERNATE SOLUTIONS

1. The lesson to be learned was not the students' about geography, but yours about honor codes. Accept the blame for the mess and give the students the grades their tests earned.

2. Throw the whole test out and forget the honor code in future tests.

3. Give the same test the next day and, this time, stay in the room and watch the students as they take it.

4. Ask your students what you should do. Let them know how disappointed you are in their behavior, but also be willing to follow their advice on a solution to the problem.

A FRIEND IN NEED . . .

Called from your room for an important telephone call during your algebra final examination, you told your students to continue with their tests and to do no talking. You were gone longer than you expected to be and returned just as the test period was ending. Four boys, including Richard, the best student in the class, were talking together as you came back into the room. They claimed, though, that they were done with their tests and gave you their papers immediately.

Skeptical, you scored their papers together and discovered enough similarity to justify your calling the boys into your room to discuss your doubts about their tests. After a short conversation three of the boys admitted that they had asked Richard for both methods and answers to four of the ten problems; Richard admitted that he had supplied this information. You decided to fail all four boys, asserting that the giving of aid in an examination is as deserving of punishment as the receiving of it.

Only in Richard's case does the "F" on the final make a significant difference in the yearly average: It drops him from an "A" to a "C." But, before turning in the grades, you discuss the problem with some of your fellow teachers and you now are wondering if you made the right decision. A guidance counselor reminds you of the pressure on bright students to be "good fellows" and to share their intellectual wealth. Another teacher, one who knows Richard, argues that your action may jeopardize his chances of admission to a good college. A third suggests that the "F" is hardly an accurate indicator of Richard's achievement on the final examination. You must agree, since Richard's final exam was a perfect paper. This teacher then goes on to accuse you of confusing academic progress with moral behavior.

Should you, then, do anything differently with regard to Richard's grade?

YOUR SOLUTION

YOUR REACTIONS TO THE ALTERNATE SOLUTIONS

ALTERNATE SOLUTIONS

1. Do as you had planned. Fail Richard, letting him know that the reason he failed the exam is that he cheated.

2. Give Richard the "A" his test would have received had he not given information to the other boys. But also tell him how displeased you are.

3. Give Richard a grade ("C" or "D") on the final examination that will drop his over-all average to a "B" instead of a "C."

CHEATING

Devoting an entire chapter of this volume to cheating may seem to some to give that topic a disproportionate importance in the life of the teacher. Yet cheating does occur in our secondary schools (and in our elementary schools and colleges, as well) and probably to a degree we shall never accurately determine. And this cheating causes problems for the classroom teacher. Cheating is also closely bound to such other aspects of the teaching/learning situation as motivation, evaluation, and discipline. Some consideration of the causes and prevention of cheating is, therefore, in order in a book like this one.

The reasons why students cheat are numerous and diverse, but often there is a common kind of cause: external pressure. Because of pressure from one source or another or from a combination of sources, the student feels he must get an assignment in, pass a particular test, or achieve a certain grade, even if to do so means he must cheat. Not infrequently the source of this pressure is a parental demand that the student succeed in school. The parents, for example, want their son to go to a certain college, or to college period, and think (rightly or wrongly) that their son must make a certain grade point average to get there. In some instances, unfortunately, the demands made by such parents call for higher achievement than their son is capable of; the son looks upon cheating as his only way out.

Sometimes parents quite unknowingly contribute to the sort of pressure that results in cheating by offering tangible rewards for grades only, and not for learning or for doing as well as one can. The father who gives his son a five-dollar bill for each "A" or dangles before him the keys to the family car contingent upon his earning a place on the honor roll may be doing so with only the worthiest of motives in mind: those of praise. Yet he is putting all his praise on the grades and none on how they are earned. His boy may well feel that the risks of cheating are worth the candle.

The opposite side of this praise coin is punishment. The parent who threatens his son with untold difficulties for doing less well than father deems satisfactory may be fostering a need to cheat on the part of that son. In fact, if the son believes that the proposed punishment is unduly severe, he may even look upon cheating as having a certain justification.

The school itself can be the source of pressures that result in a student's thinking of cheating as his only salvation. Athletic squads, for example, almost always require the maintaining of a certain grade average if a player is going to remain eligible for the team. It may seem rather ironic that the athlete would cheat in his school work to remain in an activity the avowed purpose of which is to give him a taste of true sportsmanship, but such is occasionally the case.

Peer pressure can cause some students to resort to cheating. If a student feels that his remaining a part of the social group, the clique, he wants to associate with means that he must achieve a certain grade, he may cheat to get that grade. Sometimes the act of cheating, or the participation in a group cheating enterprise, is itself a means of increasing a student's status with a peer group. His retelling for his friends how he put one over on "teach" may earn him an eminence in the group that he cannot attain with more educationally approved activities.

Whatever the source of the pressure on students to cheat, one conclusion seems clear: although cheating is a problem you must deal with when it arises, it is also likely to be symptomatic of a deeper problem that you must try not to overlook. A doctor will try to lower his patient's high fever, but he will also try to discover what it is that is causing the fever in the first place. Similarly should you try to discover what kind of pressure it is that is causing a student of yours to cheat. The reason for this is obvious. If you merely attack the outward manifestation—the incident of cheating—without exploration of how you can help with the root problem that is causing the cheating, you may run the risk of having a student who continues to cheat, but does so now in ways more likely to escape your detection. On the other hand, if you demonstrate a sincere and sympathetic willingness to help the student who cheats withstand the pressure that is causing him to cheat, you may be solving both his problem—the pressure—and yours—his cheating.

To deal with a specific example, let us consider the case of the student who cheats because his parents, for whatever reasons, make demands upon him that he feels he can satisfy only by cheating. If you discover that he has cheated in your class and then discover that parental pressure is at least part of the cause, merely informing him of your knowledge and offering to help may go a long way toward effecting the kind of solution you want. This may be the sort of case in which you want to involve the student's high school counselor; you may even want to talk with his parents. It is possible that you may be able to create a situation in which the student will work harder for you, will succeed on a level satisfactory to his now more understanding parents, and will assuredly be happier in school.

You may have noticed in the foregoing example the implicit assumption that the student could have succeeded had he applied himself properly. One of the things teachers find to be almost inevitably the case in the instances of cheating they encounter is that those students who cheat could, if they chose, do reasonably good work. The cheater is often the "B" student who wants an "A," the "C" student who wants a "B." Rare is the cheater an "F" student who just wants to pass, strange as that may seem. (It ought not to be too difficult to understand, though, when you consider that the "F" student has been recognized as one of limited ability and achievement long before he has reached secondary school. The pressures that his brighter classmates face seldom bother him. He does not have to worry about college admissions policies, his parents are more concerned about his finishing high school than about his making the honor roll, his peer group accepts or does not accept him for qualities other than academic ones.) Your task, therefore, is to provide the cheater with opportunities and encouragement to do well in your course without cheating, to do the work of which he is capable.

Such a plan suggests more attention to planning for the future of the cheater than to punishing his act of cheating. (You may recall that this same principle of trying more to effect changed future behavior than to punish past misdeeds was enunciated in the chapter on classroom discipline.) The occasion of cheating may, of course, demand some sort of punishment, but it should be a considered, as opposed to a rash, punishment. There is seldom very much to be gained but much to be lost by your marching down the aisle during a test, snatching a paper from a student who is cowering in fear of your charge, and then dramatically tearing that paper into confetti. Such a demonstration will not necessarily serve to make the other students cheat any the less and it will assure you of the undying enmity of the student whom you so unnecessarily embarrassed.

A far better way to handle this kind of situation is to shake your head knowingly during the test whenever the student looks at you. And look at you he will. A student who is cheating on a test or who is contemplating cheating always looks first, and often thereafter, at the teacher to see if the coast is clear. The student will read your headshake loud and clear. If, in your judgment, his cheating has been excessive, you can fail him for the test. If you instead think he has copied only one or two items of many on the test, you might choose to ignore the incident altogether in your grading, hoping that your letting the student off the hook will have the effect on him that will cause a changed future behavior, one that does not include cheating on tests. In either instance, however, a short, private, and informal conference is probably a good idea, for, in such a meeting, you can explore the "why" of the cheating, the pressure that causes the student to cheat in the first place.

This instance above, though, does not take into account another kind of cheating, one that is rather common and difficult to detect: copied homework assignments. The student who borrows and copies another's homework is cheating as surely as if he peeked at answers during a test situation. (The student from whom he borrows and then copies is, according to many teachers, cheating, too, but his special case will be discussed below.) To the degree that homework is a major part of the course, to that degree is this cheating an important concern of the teacher. If homework is, as it should be, mostly for the student's benefit, then the cheating is really hurting the student. This position, by the way, that cheating only hurts those who cheat is often rejected by adolescents who see the cheating as a means of escaping from the pressures mentioned above. In this instance, however, the student who copies his homework from another student is truly hurting himself. His case may be difficult for you to discover, especially if he is clever enough to change a few of the answers. One check of whether someone is cheating on homework is to compare the test performance with the homework performance. If there is a marked deviance in favor of the latter, this may be taken as a first indication that a student may be getting help (not necessarily the same as cheating) on his homework that he is not able to duplicate on tests. Such evidence can lead to further detection on your part.

A possibly better preventative procedure is rarely to require homework for grading purposes. If most of your homework assignments are understood by your students to be given for their benefit as learning devices, but not grading instruments, students will feel under no pressure to do them solely for grades; rather, they will do them for the benefits they can derive from them.

Some attention also must be given to an aspect of cheating often not even thought of as dishonest by those who engage in it. I am referring to plagiarism. Students (and some teachers, too) often regard the encyclopedia as the fount of all wisdom and, when given an assignment which involves research, copy it almost verbatim. Many do so without realizing that they are as guilty as if they copied from a fellow student. If in your teaching you require written reports on material that can be found in reference books, you would be wise to explain the proper use of such books; at the same time you could explain what plagiarism is and how students can avoid the practice.

In fact, this kind of preventative philosophy with regard to all possible situations that can result in cheating may lessen the incidence of cheating and, hence, your having to worry about it. The most desirable characteristic of such a posture is one indicative of your trust in the students. Letting them know that you are aware that many of them are under great pressure to do well in your course but that you hope they will not feel the need to cheat to alleviate this pressure may win you sufficient respect that cheating will not occur. When tests are being given, it is usually unwise to become either a head-in-the-sand ostrich around whom your students can cheat at will or an eagle-eyed martinet who watches every raised eyebrow with Gestapo-like suspicion. Walking around the room once in a while, especially if, in so doing, you can call attention to a student's failure to put his name on the paper and, thus, seem to give another reason for your wanderings, can serve to alert your students to your presence, yet not give them reason to resent that presence. An occasional glance around the room will probably suffice after that.

One aspect of cheating hinted at earlier in this discussion is that of the bright student who gives his work to someone else. Honor codes used in some schools imply that the giver of information is as guilty of wrongdoing as is the taker. Such a position seems often to ignore the rather intense peer pressure placed upon some very bright students to be "good guys" and help out those less talented or less energetic. Though able students sometimes help others simply to gain popularity, they usually do so with feelings of guilt that are far worse than any punishment you can mete out. Should you discover one of your bright students involved as the source of answers in an occurrence of cheating, try to recognize the pressures *all* the students were under when they cheated. You may choose to deal with the bright student differently from the way you deal with those who used his abilities. It behooves you to treat his case on its own merits and not to lump it under one heading you call "cheating," for, with him, both the pressures and his reactions to them may differ from those which motivated his peers.

In sum, then, cheating in its various forms can be a problem. Preventative measures and punishment that look toward the future behavior of the cheaters are likely, though, to keep both the incidence and the severity of the problem at a minimum and thus permit both the teacher and the students to get on with the tasks of teaching and learning.

FOR FURTHER READING

Byers, P. R., "What Can Be Done About Cheating?" *Illinois Education*, 56, Sept. 1967, 34-35.

Cadbury, W. E., Jr., "Self-scheduled Examinations under an Honor System," *School and Society*, Feb. 5, 1966, 68-70.

Clark, Leonard H., and Irving S. Starr, *Secondary School Teaching Methods* (2nd ed.), Chap. 11. New York: The Macmillan Company, 1967.

Dabney, V. E., "Cheating Can Be Stopped," *Saturday Review*, May 21, 1966, 68-69.

Grambs, Jean D., William J. Iverson, and Frank Patterson, *Modern Methods in Secondary Education* (rev. ed.), Chaps. 15 and 17. New York: The Dryden Press, 1958.

Johnson, R. E., and M. S. Klores, "Attitudes toward Cheating as a Function of Classroom Dissatisfaction and Peer Norms," *Journal of Educational Research*, 62, Oct. 1964, 60-64.

Knowlton, J. Q., and L. A. Hamerlynck, "Perception of Deviant Behavior: A Study of Cheating," *Journal of Educational Psychology*, 58, Dec. 1967, 379-85.

CHAPTER SIX

The Teacher and Extraclass Activities

IT'S THE SPIRITS OF THE THING

As the sponsor of the school's French Club, you agreed with the officers to hold one of your meetings at a member's house during the evening hours. The parents of the student had been to France the summer before and were going to show films of their trip. The evening meeting had all the marks of a truly valuable learning activity for the students in the club.

And learn they did, though you were put in a most difficult situation. To lend authenticity to his travelogue, the father of your club member brought out several bottles of good French wine and served wine to the students and to you. Drinking, you know, is commonplace enough in this affluent suburb where you teach, and teachers who drink are not frowned upon, but the school does have strict rules about student drinking at school events. And this evening meeting is a school event.

Yet the father is the most gracious of hosts and apparently sees nothing amiss in his serving wine. You have noticed several of the students, especially the freshmen and sophmores, glance a bit apprehensively at you as they hold out their glasses for refills.

You wonder if you ought to take some action, now or later. You are certain that word of the drinking will get back to the school principal and that he would have grounds for censuring your failing to act. Yet the father is an influential local citizen and a strong supporter of the school; he might take offense at your stopping what he believes to be an appropriate activity.

Meanwhile, said host is asking if you'll have another glass.

YOUR SOLUTION

YOUR REACTIONS TO THE ALTERNATE SOLUTIONS

ALTERNATE SOLUTIONS

1. Even though the students have had some wine, you'd better put a stop to further drinking, even if you do risk offending the host.

2. Go to your principal first thing in the morning and tell him what happened. Tell him that you finally decided to let the drinking continue.

3. Drink your wine, enjoy yourself, and don't say anything unless the principal raises the subject with you. If he does, explain what happened and why you acted as you did.

4. At the party tell the students not to drink any more unless they think their parents would approve.

THE ATHLETIC MUSICIAN OR THE MUSICAL ATHLETE?

In the small school in which you are completing your first year as band director it seems that the students who are the most capable in one activity are the most capable in some other activities. Larry is a case in point. Your best trumpeter, he is also a good student, an officer in the student government, and a first-rate athlete.

So far Larry's diverse interests and activities may have caused him some problems, but they haven't caused you any. But there's a lulu coming up this Saturday. It's the day of your district band contest and your only hope for any "first" awards is in the trumpet trio competition; Larry is the best player in your trio. There is also an outside chance that Larry might receive a first in the solo division.

But Saturday is also the day of the district track meet and Larry is a vital member of the relay team and also an outstanding dash man. The track coach told you that he wants Larry at the track meet. You replied that you wanted him at the band contest. Neither of you wants to put the boy into the middle of this situation, but you're not sure how you can avoid it.

What are you going to do?

YOUR SOLUTION

YOUR REACTIONS TO THE ALTERNATE SOLUTIONS

ALTERNATE SOLUTIONS

1. Go to the principal with your (and Larry's) dilemma and let him decide which event holds the greater importance for Larry and for the school. Insist that Larry abide by his decision.
2. Put the question to Larry and let him decide. Try to persuade the track coach that neither you nor he should put any pressure on Larry.
3. Offer to flip a coin with the track coach: Winner take all, which includes Larry.

IS YOUR MONEY WHERE YOUR MOUTH IS?

Your first year of coaching basketball has been a highly successful one, both in terms of the won-lost performance of your team and with regard to what it has learned about basketball, sportsmanship, and teamwork. Even the principal complimented you on how well the team has done and added that, with tournament time approaching, yours is a rare opportunity to use basketball as the vehicle for really upgrading the school spirit. He further suggested that some success in the state tournament could be instrumental in aiding the passage of the upcoming tax referendum to provide increased support for the school.

Today, however, just three days before the first tournament game, you are faced with a significant decision. Mr. Klein, a history teacher whose vehement opposition to basketball is known throughout the school, came to you and reported that he had seen Mark, your superstar, at a country club dinner with his parents. Along with his parents, Mark had had one cocktail before dinner. Mr. Klein does not suggest that you remove Mark from the team, but even he is probably aware of your much stated training rule that drinking or smoking will cause a boy to be dropped from the team. You have had no occasion until now to enforce the rule and even now wonder if you should. Mark was, after all, with his parents, who should be his guardians on such matters as drinking. His being dropped from the team would almost surely mean a tournament loss and would certainly have a decisive effect on the student body and the community. You think also, with some irony, of the football season when the coach had no training rules and his team was called the "Inebriated Eleven."

Still, Mark did take a drink and your rules were loud and clear. What are you going to do?

YOUR SOLUTION

YOUR REACTIONS TO THE ALTERNATE SOLUTIONS

ALTERNATE SOLUTIONS

1. Tell Mr. Klein that, since Mark was with his parents who apparently condone his drinking, you're not going to remove him from the team. Ask Mr. Klein not to say anything as your inaction might be misunderstood.

2. You have no choice. Drop Mark from the team immediately.

3. Talk with the principal about the incident and solicit and follow his advice.

4. Check with Mark to see if, in fact, he had been drinking and, if so, ask him what *he* thinks you should do.

5. Thank Mr. Klein for his information and also for his interest in basketball, but don't do anything about Mark. Let him play.

EXTRACLASS ACTIVITIES

The extraclass activities program of the typical secondary school provides much more than an opportunity for students to participate in football or debate. In many instances it determines the tone of the school, that intangible referred to as its "school spirit." And this school spirit has implications that go far beyond the "rah-rah" at the basketball game: when students and faculty have pride in their school and its accomplishments—academic, athletic, forensic, musical, governmental, social—the whole enterprise is likely to function better than in a school in which the total spirit is weak or is supportive of only one or two aspects of the school program. Because of its importance you owe some consideration to your role as a member of a faculty whose total responsibilities must include the extraclass activities program.

The scope of any school's activities program depends on some factors peculiar to the school (bobsledding is not popular in Texas schools), but its purpose, its *raison d'etre* is generally the same from district to district: to provide learning opportunities for students which are not always available in the credit course program of the school. Indeed, the existence of these opportunities is what keeps some students in school who would otherwise drop out. Boys, for example, often remain in school because their participation in the sports program provides them with satisfactions they are unable to secure in the academic program.

There are many kinds of extraclass activities. It is usually the athletic portion of the extraclass activities program that secures the greatest amount of student participation (as players, cheerleaders, and spectators) and commands the most attention from students and community alike. A winning football team, a state championship tennis squad, even an outstanding performer in an individual track event can greatly enhance a student body's sense of togetherness, its spirit. The musical activities of a school, its bands and orchestras and choruses, give talented students the chance to secure capable instruction and to perform before large groups of spectators. Speech and drama activities range from individual speeches to full-scale productions of difficult plays. The academic clubs, such as the math club or the creative writing group, permit students with similar academic interests and talents to pursue these in an after-hours setting that lacks the pressure often found in the classroom. Student government activities offer leadership and organization opportunities that can be as complex and demanding as those encountered in adult life. School dances, class parties, and the like give students an opportunity to gain some of the social graces they will need as adults.

The foregoing descriptions may have seemed but a statement of the obvious to anyone who has been in a secondary school, but it ought also to serve as a reminder of the importance of the extraclass activities program. Conducted properly, this program is one in which students can and do learn. For example, most of the extraclass activities demand team or group effort not found in the typical classroom, where the emphasis is usually (though not always rightly) placed on individual performance. Students learn something of the values of cooperation, of sportsmanship, of teamwork, and these are not to be belittled in an age as complex as ours, where the tasks of life often demand a corporate undertaking. Students in the extraclass activities program can develop increased proficiencies in areas of their interests. The student poet, for example, cannot write poetry all the time in English class, but can work further on his writing in the after-hours English club. Decorating for the prom or selling tickets for it may have significant relevance in later years for the future director of the community club social. The boy who plays golf or tennis in high school is learning a game that he can play for the rest of his life. Students also can acquire a sense of responsibility for their own behavior, for the success of their efforts in the extraclass activities program; in the traditional classroom, decisions and evaluations usually reside with the teacher (again perhaps not rightly).

As a classroom teacher whose primary interests naturally lie in the subject you are employed to teach, where do you fit into the extraclass activities program? Unfortunately, many secondary school teachers give only grudging support to extraclass activities. They view chaperoning a dance or sponsoring a club as onerous duties, extra burdens placed on them by a school administration too tight or too unsophisticated to devise other means of handling such activities. They may do their fair share of this extra work, but certainly no more than that, and even that not willingly. Other teachers, however, see in the extraclass activities program the same kinds of opportunities that exist for students. Athletic coaches, choir directors, drama teachers often get their greatest rewards and their most pronounced successes from their efforts in the extraclass activities program. The rewards, by the way, are seldom financial, as the pay for the long hours of coaching a team or directing a dramatics production is frequently at a level that makes the activity truly a labor of love.

These teachers need the help of other teachers. Someone must sell tickets at the basketball game and supervise the crowd; someone in addition to the faculty adviser must chaperone the dance the Hobbies Club is sponsoring; someone must help drive the debate team to its "away" meets—these "someones" are usually teachers. Without their cooperation the extraclass activities program simply cannot function.

Your task, then, is to provide what help you are able to give. Yours may be a major role—that of coach or adviser—or a minor one—that of occasional chaperone or driver. In either instance your being willing to assist in the important extraclass activities program can contribute materially to the success of the program and *also to your success as a teacher*.

It is this second benefit that teachers unhappy with their extraclass assignments often overlook. Many teachers perform much better *in the classroom* as a direct result of their efforts out of it. You will recall that the section on motivation in Chapter Two included the prescription that you appear to your students as a person of many interests. What better way to demonstrate these interests that lie outside your teaching field than to make them apparent at school activities? The teacher who cheers at the football game, who attends the school drama events, who sponsors a club has other interests that can become obvious to the students who see him at such functions.

Students who are aware of your participation in the extraclass activities program will appreciate your efforts. Often such students take a much greater proprietary interest in the extraclass activities than in the academic classes. It is *their* prom; they chose the theme, hired the band, decorated the gym, and even prepared the intermission punch and cookies. Those teachers who help them with these tasks and who, on the big night itself, serve as chaperones are seen in a favorable light. It is not unreasonable to assume that the students who like your help with their extraclass activities will accord you a similar cooperation in your classroom.

Administrators will also appreciate your help, even though the school financial structure may prohibit their paying you anything significant for that help. The typical school principal attends far more events in the extraclass activities program than any of his teachers, but he cannot attend them all. Your willingness to help out will be welcomed.

Another important reason for your becoming a part of the extraclass activities program is that such participation enables you to get to know your students in a way you cannot possibly know them from classroom experience alone. The yearbook adviser, working regularly with his staff, develops a relationship that can become the real stuff of teaching, the interaction of adult teacher and adolescent student on a project in which both are interested. The student council adviser can nurture the leadership potential of his sergeant-at-arms until the immature boy elected to that post becomes a mature young man able to act with responsibility and judgment. In these extra activities you can come to know more of students' backgrounds, their interests and aspirations, their thoughts about matters far different from those you discuss with them in your classes. Similarly, they get to know you better.

Participation in the extraclass activities program, then, can spell the difference between the good teacher (as seen by the students) and the great teacher. Such participation can renew your feelings of optimism about the whole educational enterprise. It can aid your teaching. Indeed, it can enrich your life.

FOR FURTHER READING

Bent, Rudyard K., and Adolph Unruh, *Secondary School Curriculum,* Chap. 6. Lexington, Mass.: D. C. Heath and Company, 1969.

Blount, Nathan S., and H. J. Klausmeier, *Teaching in the Secondary School* (3rd ed.), Chap. 17. New York: Harper and Row, Publishers, 1968.

Douglas, Leonard M., *The Secondary Teacher at Work,* Chap. 15. Boston: D. C. Heath and Company, 1967.

Dumas, Wayne, and Weldon Beckner, *Introduction to Secondary Education: A Foundations Approach,* Chap. 8. Scranton, Pa.: International Textbook Company, 1968.

Frederick, Robert W., *Student Activities in American Education.* New York: The Center for Applied Research in Education, 1965.

Hand, Harold C., *Principles of Public Secondary Education,* Chap. 7. New York: Harcourt, Brace & World, Inc., 1958.

McKean, Robert C., *Principles and Methods in Secondary Education,* Chap. 10. Columbus, Ohio: Charles E. Merrill Books, Inc., 1962.

Wood, D. I., "Are Activities Programs Really Activities Programs?" *School Activities,* 39, Sept. 1967, 8-10.

CHAPTER SEVEN

The Teacher
and
Staff Relationships

CIVICS IN THE SCIENCE LAB

One of the unwritten policies for teachers at the school where you teach is that, if crowding occurs, new teachers are the first to be denied their own rooms. They become "floaters" and teach in a different room each period. Thus, in your first year, you have your five classes of civics in five different classrooms.

Four periods pose no particular problems, but the fifth more than evens the balance. That period you teach in Mrs. Smalley's science laboratory classroom. Early in the year Mrs. Smalley, an older teacher, asked if she could work at the back of the room while you taught; you were in the classroom during her one planning period, she explained. Though dubious and just a little nervous about having such an experienced teacher watching you teach, you did agree.

Generally, there have been no interruptions, although Mrs. Smalley has on occasion been noisier than you would have liked her to be. Sometimes, too, she stopped what she was doing and listened to your lesson with a quizzical expression on her face that she did not explain later. These have been on days when the lesson hasn't gone well and you have begun wondering if Mrs. Smalley questions your competence. And once she did interrupt your lesson to reprimand two students who were talking quietly. Afterwards, these students complained that they had been talking about the lesson. You said nothing to Mrs. Smalley at that time.

The last two weeks, however, have been almost impossible. Mrs. Smalley's students are doing science fair projects and she regularly lets two or three students come from their study halls to your class to do additional work. They begin quietly enough, but very soon they are talking and get louder and louder. Mrs. Smalley says nothing to them. Their experiments, too, are disruptive. Many of them use colored lights or moving parts and your students (and sometimes even you) become fascinated. But, amid the interruptions and the awe, your students are learning precious little civics.

The science fair isn't for four more weeks and you're not sure you can continue to accomplish even the very little you've accomplished these last two. But what can you do?

YOUR SOLUTION

YOUR REACTIONS TO THE ALTERNATE SOLUTIONS

ALTERNATE SOLUTIONS

1. Continue as you have been, simply putting up with the interruptions from Mrs. Smalley and her students.
2. Tell Mrs. Smalley that you can live with her working in the back of the room, but that you must ask her to keep her students out of the room during your class.
3. Go to the principal with your problem and insist that he either speak to Mrs. Smalley or find you another room.
4. Ask Mrs. Smalley if she'd mind if you'd bring a few of your students to her science class for a group discussion of civics during *your* planning period. Maybe she'll take the hint.

IS THIS RELATIONSHIP PROFESSIONAL?

One of the things Mr. Clark, your principal, dwelt on at the preschool meeting of new teachers was the necessity of a teacher's maintaining a professional relationship with all of his students. "Permitting them to use your first name or your getting too involved with their personal problems can often lead to trouble," he asserted to the assembled new teachers, among which group was Mr. Wallace.

Throughout this first year you have heard many good reports about Mr. Wallace from the senior students in your English class who also have him for senior social studies. His is a discussion class, dealing with highly sophisticated contemporary problems. You know from your own slight acquaintance with Mr. Wallace that he is intelligent and dynamic, truly a worthwhile addition to teaching in general and your school in particular.

Last Saturday night you attended a movie in a neighboring town and saw Mr. Wallace with one of the students you both teach, a very mature senior named Sharon. That it was quite obviously a date arrangement was evident by their hand holding and general displays of affection. They did not see you.

You wonder if you should say anything about this incident to anyone. After all, you think, Mr. Wallace is, like you, only twenty-one or twenty-two; Sharon is at least seventeen. Still, dating between teacher and student is strictly forbidden by Mr. Clark. At the very least Mr. Wallace would get a severe reprimand; possibly he could be fired and your school would miss his exemplary classroom talents. And what about Sharon in all of this? Perhaps you should first approach her? Or should you go to Mr. Wallace? Or to Mr. Clark? Or should you possibly just forget the whole thing?

YOUR SOLUTION

YOUR REACTIONS TO THE ALTERNATE SOLUTIONS

ALTERNATE SOLUTIONS

1. Go directly to Mr. Clark and tell him what you saw. Mr. Wallace's behavior with Sharon could give the entire teaching staff a bad name.

2. Don't do anything. What Mr. Wallace and Sharon do after school is their business.

3. Talk to Mr. Wallace, telling him that you saw him and Sharon. Argue that, as a fellow teacher, you feel compelled to try to persuade him not to date students.

4. Talk to Sharon. Let her know that you think that her behavior, if continued, could jeopardize the career of a fine teacher. Urge her to forego the dates with Mr. Wallace at least until after she graduates from high school.

A ONE-TEACHER TEAM

You were really happy with your first teaching assignment when you discovered that you would be team teaching United States History with Mr. Barnes, one of the older members of the department and a teacher with a fine reputation. It would be a double class, almost seventy students, and you thought that, with both of you there, some exciting learning could take place.

After one quarter of teaching, your enchantment has worn off. Of the forty-four days of class you, a new teacher for whom each preparation is difficult and very time-consuming, have taught twenty-seven days, Mr. Barnes only ten. The other days were spent in testing or in panel discussions or films and your recollection is that you were present on all these days. Mr. Barnes was there for only a few of them. Moreover, you have discovered that Mr. Barnes's reputation is based on his popularity, not on his ability as a teacher. In your judgment he doesn't teach well at all. He does joke a lot with the class, is glib, and requires very little work from his students. By comparison your teaching, mostly lecturing since that is the only method you think will work when you are facing, alone, over sixty-five high school juniors, is not well received. You have also had more discipline problems in this class than in any of your other sections.

You have been reluctant to say anything to Mr. Barnes or anyone else about his frequently being absent. He is the ticket manager for the school and seems to have to use the time when your class meets to handle ticket arrangements. This time is in addition to the released time he has for the job. You have learned, though, that much of his ticket managing seems to be of the sort that he can do in the teacher's lounge over coffee, for that is where he is spending much of his time when he misses your joint class. Mr. Barnes is also a good friend of both the department head and the school principal.

What has proved to be the final straw was Mr. Barnes's request this morning. Since you had done most of the teaching, he said, why don't you go ahead and average a grade for *all* the students, his as well as yours? Mr. Barnes pleaded much work with tickets for the upcoming basketball season. If you were to do as he asks, you would not only have to average the grades; you would also have to grade all of the end-of-the-quarter essay examinations.

You decide you must do something. But what?

YOUR SOLUTION

YOUR REACTIONS TO THE ALTERNATE SOLUTIONS

ALTERNATE SOLUTIONS

1. Talk to Mr. Barnes and tell him how you feel. Tell him that, whether the class learns anything or not, you are going to do only half the work. And that includes the test scoring and the grade averaging for this quarter.
2. Continue as you are, shouldering your burden in silence and resolving that next year, if you last that long, you will not team teach with Mr. Barnes.
3. Go to the department head or the principal or both and tell them of your complaint, even though you know of their friendship for Mr. Barnes.
4. Tell Mr. Barnes that you will volunteer to become an unpaid assistant ticket manager if you can have the same amount of time to devote to the task as he takes.

COUNT ME IN/OUT

Though you see your homeroom group only twenty minutes a day, you have tried to be the counselor and friend to these students which the school expects you to be. You think that you have been generally successful and have rather enjoyed the relationships you have established. You have discussed school policy with them, helped them win second place in the homecoming float contest, and tried to be of whatever help you could.

Today, though, you were faced with a problem you're not sure you can handle. Five of your homeroom students and three of their friends whom you don't even know came to you after school and asked for your assistance. It seems that they believe that their history teacher, Mr. Wilson, should be fired immediately. (You, a new teacher, know Mr. Wilson, an old-timer, only slightly.) If what these students report of him is true, you're inclined to agree with them. Mr. Wilson, they say, never prepares for class, does not grade any of the mountains of homework he requires, rarely talks about history in class, is very unfriendly—in short, he has very little going for him with these particular students. Would you, your students ask, either go to the principal yourself with their complaints or go with them and be their spokesman?

You explain that this could be a sensitive issue and request a few days to consider what you should do. The students grant this request and leave; their problem and how you are going to handle it remain.

What are you going to do?

YOUR SOLUTION

YOUR REACTIONS TO THE ALTERNATE SOLUTIONS

ALTERNATE SOLUTIONS

1. Tell your students that, as one of Mr. Wilson's fellow faculty members, you feel that you must not get involved. Suggest, though, that they go to Mr. Wilson and explain their grievances to him.

2. Without telling the students what you intend to do, go to Mr. Wilson yourself and tell him what was reported to you. Do not tell him who told you.

3. Again without telling your students, see the principal and tell him the story.

4. Comply with your students' request and go with them to the principal.

5. Tell your students to see the principal, but not to mention that you urged them to. Do not get involved in what is a problem that Mr. Wilson and the principal should solve.

6. Tell your students that you are going to take their case to the principal and that you will report his reactions to them.

"HE'S A GOOD TEACHER, BUT . . ."

You were a little surprised that, in your first year of teaching, you were going to have a student teacher working with you in your biology classes. And even more surprised when he showed up, for he is a Negro.

Your own attitudes include none of a prejudicial nature, but the community in which you are teaching can still recall the school desegregation bitterness and contains a good many people of both races who view each other with suspicion and hostility. Though the races have mixed in school without incidents, there have been no Negro teachers—until, that is, your student teacher, Mr. Sanders, showed up.

Fortunately, his first few weeks have gone magnificently. A fine teacher, Mr. Sanders knows his subject well, plans carefully, and presents excellent lessons. The only concern you have is that your students aren't responding as you think they should—and would if the teacher were white. There seems to be a tenseness, as though the students are waiting for Mr. Sanders to make a mistake so that they can ridicule him. You even wonder if they are not trying to create an incident that would put him in a bad light. One of your students even asked you how you, a white, liked working so closely with a Negro and seemed surprised when you answered that it didn't bother you a bit and was, in fact, most enjoyable when the teacher was as capable as Mr. Sanders.

Though Mr. Sanders knows well the community feelings, you're quite certain he is oblivious to the classroom atmosphere, one you think could explode at any time. It may be, however, that you are seeing problems where they do not exist.

You wonder, therefore, if you should take any action and, if so, what.

YOUR SOLUTION

YOUR REACTIONS TO THE ALTERNATE SOLUTIONS

ALTERNATE SOLUTIONS

1. Do nothing, hoping that the situation you fear will not erupt. But do keep a close eye on things.

2. Talk to Mr. Sanders, explaining your fears to him and alerting him to what you think might happen.

3. Talk privately with members of the class, exploring their feelings and making sure they understand yours.

4. Openly praise Mr. Sanders to your class. Let them know how fortunate you think they are that they have such an able student teacher.

BASEBALL, YES; GEOMETRY, NO

Jerry is supposed to be as good in baseball as he is bad in math. The first semester he earned a squeaky "C" from you that was as much gift as grade. Because of the cumulative nature of mathematics, Jerry's work this semester has hovered between a "D" and an "F." Yet he is in geometry, the only senior in a course designed for sophomores. You know that he is taking the course only to meet college requirements, for Jerry is an extraordinary baseball player and apparently stands a good chance of receiving a full scholarship—if, that is, he passes geometry. Ironically, though, it is his baseball that is helping create the geometry difficulties. In each of the first few weeks of the season he has missed at least two, and once four, class meetings because the "away" baseball games have taken him away from school the last period when your geometry class meets.

You can't really fault Jerry. He has made a pretty good gesture of trying. At your invitation he came in early a couple of mornings for extra help, but soon that work ended because he had to report for preschool baseball practice. He always obtains the assignments for the days he misses and gets something handed in, though that something sometimes bears little resemblance to a good geometry lesson.

Yes, Jerry is okay in your book, but not so his coach, Mr. Wickens, who today interrupted your third hour algebra class because that was the "only time" he could see you. His inquiry about Jerry's progress was a bit brusque, but mild indeed compared with his outburst when you informed him that Jerry might fail the course. In no uncertain terms he told you that Jerry "had blamed well better pass geometry," that his getting a scholarship hinged on his getting at least a "C," and that, if Jerry didn't get a "C," he (Mr. Wickens) would personally talk to the principal about your competence.

When he left, you were as mad as he was and wondered what, if any, steps you should take about what you regard as his completely unprofessional behavior.

YOUR SOLUTION

YOUR REACTIONS TO THE ALTERNATE SOLUTIONS

ALTERNATE SOLUTIONS

1. Tell the principal what you think of Mr. Wickens' competence. Explain that you believe that you deserve an apology from the baseball coach.

2. Forget all about your conversation with Mr. Wickens. Give Jerry whatever grade he earns.

3. Tell Jerry about your displeasure with Mr. Wickens' remarks to you. Let him know that you hope that he gets the "C," but that he'll have to merit it.

4. See Mr. Wickens again and tell him that you think Jerry can pass provided that he can be in your class every day (meaning he'll miss, or be late for, the "away" games) and can come in every morning for the extra help you're willing to give him (meaning that he'll miss the morning practice sessions).

STAFF RELATIONSHIPS

The development of satisfactory relationships with those with whom you work is one of the most crucial aspects of your life as a teacher. The education of youth is a joint enterprise, demanding, if it is to be successful, a cooperative working together of all those adults engaged in the venture. No teacher can operate in a vacuum, though some teachers behave as if they wished that they could. Instead, teachers must cooperate with others in their departments, with those in other departments, with the administrative and guidance staffs of the school, and even with the non-professional personnel to insure that conditions for student learning remain as favorable as they can be.

The group with whom you will work most closely is the department, those other teachers in the school who teach the same subject you do, though perhaps on different year- or ability-levels. With these people you try to develop subject matter sequences that permit you to see how your subject, say English II or geometry, fits into the total school program in English or mathematics. With them also you can examine new teaching materials and practices, can share instructional tools and techniques, can discuss problems pertinent to the teaching of your subject. One of the important people in such a group is the department chairman, whose functions vary from school to school, but usually include the over-all management of departmental affairs. Often a master teacher of many years' experience, the department chairman can provide you with assistance that ranges from source material to classroom gimmicks; the wise novice tries to benefit from the experience and expertise of the department chairman.

Your work with teachers outside your department can also be important. In disparagement of the efficiency of committee work, one wit once described a camel as "a horse put together by a committee." Such calumny notwithstanding, your efforts in working jointly with other teachers on committees can be both interesting and beneficial. Committees of teachers are often the policy-makers of the school, and the intellectual give-and-take that precedes the formulation of decisions can be exciting and rewarding. Instead of decrying your assignment to a committee or failing to work at your best on it, as, unfortunately, too many teachers do, you should welcome these opportunities of working with your fellow teachers as a means of getting to know them (not always an easy task in large schools where faculty size can exceed 100) and of accomplishing something of use to the school.

The administrative staff of the school plays a dual role with respect to your work, one that occasionally causes both them and you some difficulty. On the one hand they are your "bosses," those people charged with the determination of your being rehired or given salary increases. On the other hand, theirs is a service role, as they help you with severe discipline problems (see Chapter Three) or assist you in teaching techniques and in securing curricular materials. The major function of the secondary school principal ought to be the improvement of the instructional program; many principals, however, abdicate this responsibility and concentrate instead on school management—budget-making, assignment of teachers, pupils, courses, and rooms—or on discipline of students. The good principal keeps close tabs on what goes on in the classroom, not as a "snoopervisor," a label he is sometimes uncharitably given, but as a means of seeing how he can assist his teachers in doing the work for which they were hired—teaching students. You hopefully will discover that your principal is a source not only of inspiration but also of ideas and techniques that you can implement in your teaching.

Where the rub comes in this dual role is that teachers become reluctant to use the service functions administrators can perform out of fear, often wholly unjustified, that to do so is to reveal a weakness that may militate against their being given a new contract or a raise. But the fact remains that the teacher who cannot manage his class, who cannot plan well what his students will learn or motivate them to learn it, who cannot evaluate fairly, does need help; more often than not that help can come from an administrator if the teacher is willing to approach him. Should you encounter problems that seem beyond your solving by yourself, consider carefully if the principal is not indeed the person you should see for help.

Another category of school employees, the guidance staff, can often be the classroom teacher's best friend. Blunt advice is perhaps best here: if you have difficulties with an individual student, do see his guidance counselor, who can, at the least, provide you with test scores and other data that may help you work with the student; the counselor may even be able to offer solutions you had not thought of. The guidance counselor is most likely to be aware if a student's home background is causing him to have problems in school, if another student's failure to make the football team is causing him to think of dropping out, if a third student's trouble with his girl friend is carrying over into his academic work. In short, the guidance staff can be an important source of help and information, one you should use.

Other specialized personnel on the school staff aid the instructional program—and, hence, your success as a teacher—in significant ways. The librarian serves not only students but also teachers—provided the teachers make him aware of their needs. He can suggest special materials that you may not even know of; he can collect books, magazines, pamphlets, for source materials on virtually any unit you choose to present; he can direct your students when they come to the library before or after school or during study halls.

Another person whose help can be valuable is the specialist in charge of audio-visual materials and equipment. Projectors of all kinds—movie, slide, opaque, overhead—and sound equipment such as record players and tape recorders today play an important role in education, and rightly so. Their proliferation in schools, as well as that of teaching machines and programmed learning materials, in no way ought to suggest that teachers face extinction in the face of mechanical monsters; rather, these machines serve as evidence that teachers are willing to try new methods and materials to enable their students to learn. Your having this positive attitude about these machines is necessary but not sufficient: You must also know what aids exist in your school, how you can operate them, and what classroom uses you can make of them. For help in these concerns the A-V specialist is indispensable.

A third school specialist whose work enables you to do yours better is the school nurse. When a student needs special consideration in your classroom because of a physical impairment (for example, the hard of hearing or poorly sighted child who needs special placement near the front of the room), the nurse can provide you the appropriate information. Certainly the nurse is a teacher's best source of assistance when a student becomes ill during a class. Even the strongest teacher gets a fluttery stomach when a student faints or vomits in the classroom; thankfully, these emergencies occur rarely, but when they do the teacher wants to know how to get the nurse in the shortest possible time.

Some large districts employ other specialized persons whose assistance you should make use of when appropriate. Curriculum coordinators and subject matter supervisors can help you with the "What" of your teaching; their work includes their keeping abreast of the latest in materials and methods, knowledge of which they can and will pass along to you. School psychologists and social workers, remedial reading specialists, home visitation teachers can help with the students you teach. They can work with those students whose special needs require time and skill you do not have. Too often, these specialists are regarded by the very teachers whose best interests they daily serve as so many administrative "pen pushers," people who really help little in the day-to-day routine of the schools. A more wholesome and, in the vast majority of school districts fortunate enough to be able to secure such people, a more realistic view is that these people and their special competencies are to be welcomed. They can provide services that can soon become a part of the repertory of helps available to every teacher.

The whole point of this chapter is that education is a cooperative endeavor. Your securing help from your fellow workers depends in part upon your asking for it; it also depends on your being willing to cooperate with your fellow workers. And many are the tasks you can perform without possessing any more skills than you left college with. In the typical school, dances must be chaperoned, special trips or school buses must be supervised, Saturday football tickets must be sold. Your uncomplaining acceptance of these not always pleasant duties will be repaid in kind with the cooperation of your colleagues. (When all teachers share in these extra tasks, the burden on any one teacher is lightened and the whole school functions better.) You can also keep other staff members—principals, guidance workers, nurses—informed of special things you learn about students that these people can use in their work.

One more pressing reason for staff cooperation lies in an instructional arrangement that seems likely to become even more common than it presently is. More and more schools are examining how best they can implement team teaching in their programs. If you find yourself in a team teaching arrangement, the need for cooperation will be obvious. Teams of teachers presently report that the biggest hurdle to success in their work rests in the amount of cooperation they can effect. When the team members share fully in the efforts, each doing his assigned task as effectively as he can do it, good teaching is likely to result. Conversely, a team whose members suspect each other of malingering or of incompetence often becomes an actual detriment to the school instructional program. Team teaching, therefore, requires a special degree of joint effort, but it is of the same kind that must pervade the entire school if its students are to be taught well.

FOR FURTHER READING

Bush, Robert N., and Dwight W. Allen, *A New Design for High School Education,* Chaps. 5 and 10. New York: McGraw-Hill Book Company, 1964.

Drayer, Adam M., *Problems and Methods in High School Teaching,* Chap. 6. Boston: D. C. Heath and Company, 1963.

Dumas, Wayne, and Weldon Beckner, *Introduction to Secondary Education: A Foundations Approach,* Chap. 13. Scranton, Pa.: International Textbook Company, 1968.

Inlow, Gail M., *Maturity in High School Teaching,* Chap. 2. Englewood Cliffs, N. J.: Prentice-Hall, Inc., 1963.

McKean, Robert C. *Principles and Methods in Secondary Education,* Chap. 12. Columbus, Ohio: Charles E. Merrill Books, Inc., 1962.

Mulford, Ann, "What Makes Teachers Burn?" *NEA Journal,* 50, May 1966, 13-15.

Oliva, Peter F., and Ralph A. Scrafford, *Teaching in a Modern Secondary School,* Chap. 17. Columbus, Ohio: Charles E. Merrill Books, Inc., 1965.

Petersen, Carl H., "Team Teaching in the High School," *Education,* 50, Feb. 1965, 342-47.

Trump, J. Lloyd, and Delmas F. Miller, *Secondary School Curriculum Improvement,* Chap. 24. Boston: Allyn and Bacon, Inc., 1968.